How to
and N

Rosemary Low

This Book Belongs to

....

....

John Bartholomew & Son Ltd.
Edinburgh

First Published in Great Britain by
John Bartholomew & Son Ltd.,
12 Duncan Street, Edinburgh, EH9 1TA

ISBN 0 7028 1029 0

British Library Cataloguing in Publication Data
Low, Rosemary
How to keep parrots, cockatiels and macaws in cage or aviary.
1. Parrots
I. Title
636.6'865   SF473.P3

ISBN 0 7028 1029 0

Printed in Great Britain by
John Bartholomew & Son Ltd.

Contents

Introduction

Parrots are fascinating to man. There is perhaps no group of birds in the whole avian kingdom which is better known, better loved and more universally kept for sheer enjoyment.

But before embarking on the purchase of parrots for pets, or for the interest which breeding them brings, some thought should be given to whether the best conditions can be provided to keep them healthy and happy.

This book describes their requirements under captive conditions and how best to fulfil them. It emphasises how to breed them or to create the conditions necessary to persuade them to rear young for, increasingly, in this conservation-minded age, the awareness has spread that merely *keeping* birds is not enough. A single bird, cherished as a pet, has brought years of enjoyment to many people, and this is another aspect entirely. Both are explored in the pages which follow.

Starting With Parrots

Parrots are among the most interesting and rewarding birds it is possible to keep; they are intelligent, affectionate, playful, lively and colourful. However, they can also be noisy and demanding – in terms of time and attention – and these points must be borne in mind before the decision is made to start keeping parrots. Tame birds are especially demanding and if they do not receive sufficient attention they will develop undesirable habits, such as screaming or feather plucking. Tame cockatoos and macaws can be almost unbelievably time-consuming and are therefore suitable only for those who are at home during the day. Intelligent birds such as these and the African Grey Parrot will become bored and lonely if left alone for long periods each day.

Those with the desire to keep parrots but without the time to devote to a tame bird should consider building an aviary, either indoors or outdoors, and perhaps obtain a pair of one of the larger species. They will provide their owner with unlimited enjoyment and may even rear young. Breeding parrots provides an enormous sense of satisfaction and also helps to meet the demand for these birds now that far fewer are imported from their countries of origin. If breeding is the main aim, it is advisable to start with easily bred species such as Cockatiels and certain Australian parakeets, rather than the larger birds which are seldom prolific or easy to breed.

Their prolificacy has made Cockatiels, lovebirds and Australian parakeets the most popular birds with aviculturists, and among the lowest in price. They are therefore suitable birds for the beginner. There are several important reasons why it is advisable to start off with young birds obtained from the breeder. Young birds settle down under new management more easily than do adults; in fact, a veterinary surgeon who carries out large numbers of post-mortem examinations on parrots from private collections has found that death in parakeets and lovebirds shortly after removal to a new home is extremely common.

For breeding purposes young birds are less of a risk. One can seldom be certain that adult birds have not been sold because they were unsatisfactory breeders or failed to breed. Almost equally important, especially in species in which male and female are not quickly compatible, is that pairs are more likely to be compatible if they grow up together. There will be none of the bloodshed which sometimes follows the introduction of adult birds.

Young birds can easily be trained to sample various foods and this is important for potential breeding stock. Most breeders have their preferred rearing foods, which an adult bird from an outside source may refuse to sample.

An obvious advantage of buying first year birds is that one knows their age. Once a parrot of any kind has moulted into adult plumage there is no way of determining its age.

The most apparent disadvantage of obtaining young birds is that the purchaser will have to wait one or two years before the bird is old enough to breed. However, even this can be an advantage for the beginner, as he has time to learn the birds' habits and preferences before they start to rear their young.

When buying a bird of any kind it should be examined closely for signs of ill health. Even those who have previously had no experience of birds will be aware that one which spends much time sleeping (and it should be noted that healthy adult birds normally sleep on one foot), has plumage which is ruffled rather than sleek (some adult birds normally have the head feathers ruffled although the body plumage is sleek), and has the eyes dull and sunken, rather than bright and alert, is not in good health.

The plumage should be inspected for certain features which indicate that the bird is not in perfect health. Young aviary-bred parakeets which have the flight and/or tail feathers missing or poorly formed, may be suffering from French moult, a problem which is common in budgerigars. Its cause is not known although there are countless theories on the subject. Some affected birds recover, others never grow flight and tail feathers.

A more serious feather condition which is particularly common in cockatoos, and has been known in other parrots, has caused months or years of distress to countless owners of cockatoos. For this reason only cockatoos in perfect feather should be bought. This disease, which is almost certainly caused by a deficiency in the diet, often becomes evident at the bird's first or second moult in captivity. The new feathers are very weak and break off when the bird attempts to preen them; crest feathers grow and fall out and tail and flight feathers eventually are entirely lacking. Numerous cures have been tried but probably the only one which has succeeded—but not in all birds treated—is the daily addition of sea salt to the drinking water. Possibly it contains a trace mineral

Pale-headed Rosella cock and hen

Stanley Rosella
Cock (left), Hen (right)

9

which is lacking in the diet of affected birds.

Imported parrots, especially the larger species, often have the primary feathers of one wing cut. Unless this has been carried out inexpertly the feathers will grow again, thus cut wings should not deter the buyer. It is worth pointing out that parrots are capable of flight even though they may have only one primary feather in each wing. Neglecting to watch the growth of new flight feathers has been the cause of countless escapes of tame parrots whose owners were quite unaware that their birds could fly.

When buying a parrot for a pet, most people will want to obtain a young bird which will become tame and perhaps learn to talk. Genuine talking parrots are seldom offered for sale, thus the only alternative is to buy a young bird and train it. Unfortunately, the most common mistake is in buying a bird which is too old. Beware of the seller who informs that a parrot is about 18 months old, which is another way of saying: 'It is older than a year but I don't know how old'. In the true, or short-tailed parrots, young birds can be indentified by their eye colour. When they are in the region of one year this changes from dark grey or black. In adult Grey Parrots the iris is yellow; and in adult Amazon parrots it is usually orange, but varies with the species. All young parrots have the colour of the iris different to that of the adult, and in small species adult eye colour is obtained at a few months old.

As a general guide, the plumage is usually less bright in young birds, but this is not always true. The feet will have a smooth appearance, compared with the more horny look of adult birds. In young Grey Parrots, for example, the tail is a duller, darker red than the bright scarlet of the adult.

Young macaws can be distinguished by their eye colour and by their shorter tails. In cockatoos, unless extremely young indeed (in which case the beak will be pinkish and fleshy and they will be calling to be fed), young birds are not readily distinguished from adults; they have the eye greyish-black, hardly differing from that of some adults.

When buying a pet bird it is wise to avoid those which are extremely nervous; while they may become tame eventually, the process can take months. It is worth prolonging the search for a suitable bird because many young parrots are imported which are fairly tame and steady on arrival.

The choice of a pet bird is never easy, not only because the many species vary so much in their suitability, but because individuals of those species have widely differing temperaments and personalities. However, there are a few points which should be borne in mind before the choice is made. Macaws, cockatoos (especially the large species) and Amazon parrots are very noisy birds which have regular periods of screaming, usually early in the morning and during the evening. Unless one is prepared for this—and has neighbours who will tolerate what can be a most unpleasant and irritating sound—keeping one of these birds should not be contemplated. One can no more prevent them from screaming than one can prevent a dog barking; some individuals are worse than others and will be difficult for the fondest owner to tolerate inside a house. In any case, most large parrots are far better off in an aviary, except in the rare case of a very tame bird whose owner has unlimited time to spend with it.

Many of those contemplating buying a parrot for a pet are bewildered by the choice of species available. A few suggestions may prove helpful. Those who have young children should avoid the larger species which can inflict a very painful bite; even the most gentle bird will retaliate if teased. There can be no more charming pet for the household with a young family than a Cockatiel. These birds are extremely easy to tame and to teach to talk, they are long-lived and inexpensive. Cockatiels fulfil the requirements of a tame and friendly pet and are more suitable for the average household than most of the larger species. It is a pity that these birds are overlooked by many who spend large sums on birds which are highly unsuitable.

Many people want to own a tame parrot because they are fascinated by their ability to mimic, and they invariably ask which species makes the best talker. There is little doubt that there is nothing to equal the talents of a Grey Parrot. Not only do some individuals accumulate a huge repertoire of words, but all Greys can reproduce most faithfully the *tone* of voice so that one is never left in doubt as to which member of the family was the teacher. They also have a facility for imitating the sounds around them which can be less fortunate if they decide to reproduce such sounds as a squeaking door or a dog barking, or downright annoying if they can copy the ring of the telephone with such accuracy that from a distance one cannot detect whether the sound comes from bell or bird!

Some Greys become very tame but others always remain aloof, to the disappointment of their owner who had hoped for a friendly pet. However, Greys are extremely intelligent and they are very seldom as noisy as most large parrots, being more inclined to whistle than to shriek. Often they are one-man birds and attach themselves very firmly to one member of a household. Many of the larger parrots show a preference for people of one sex and will never tolerate the attentions of the other.

If obtained when young, macaws and Amazon parrots readily become tame. With the exception of a few species of Amazons, such as the Yellow-naped and Yellow-fronted, these birds are seldom talented talkers but most acquire a vocabulary of a few words whether or not any conscious effort is made to teach them to talk. Few cockatoos acquire an extensive vocabulary, but this is compensated for by the extremely affectionate nature of many birds. However, others never become tame and indeed some are so nervous that it is unkind to cage them. Such birds are suitable only for an aviary.

Some of the smaller parrots, including the many conures from South and Central America, make charming pets if obtained when young. Their main fault is their harsh voices.

It is often extremely difficult to resist buying a bird on impulse, especially if it is young and tame. But the wise buyer will read as much as he or she can about the species before making a purchase. An appendix at the end of this book gives details of further reading. Advice can also be sought from experienced aviculturists; the secretary of a cage bird or foreign bird society will usually be most helpful in providing the names of such people.

Aviaries and Cages

Whether parrots are to be housed indoors or out, in cages or aviaries, a good deal of thought should be given to their accommodation because initial mistakes, especially in the case of aviaries, will prove expensive to rectify. Aviaries are the best way of housing birds for breeding purposes—and many parrots have bred successfully in indoor aviaries, so those who do not have outdoor accommodation need not entirely give up the idea of breeding these birds.

Most breeders will start off in a modest way with perhaps between three and six pairs of birds. The most usual mistake is in trying to house more than one pair together or mixing them with other types of birds, such as finches. This often occurs when the fancier already keeps the smaller species and decides to take up parakeets. However, unless he is prepared to provide a range of aviaries for them he should think again. Most members of the parrot family are too aggressive or spiteful to keep with other birds. There are exceptions, the main one being the Cockatiel which usually proves inoffensive when kept with any other birds, even the very smallest seed-eater. Also, in large aviaries there is more chance of different species living together compatibly and even breeding, but there is a large element of risk in this practice. Birds which previously proved perfectly trustworthy have often been known to kill their companions on coming into breeding condition, or when their own young fledge.

Crimson Rosella

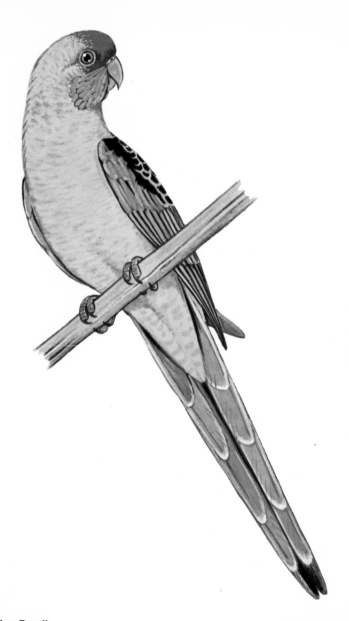

Yellow Rosella

Birdkeepers should always remember that the lives of their birds are in their hands and can be endangered by a moment's carelessness or thoughtlessness; this applies especially where mixing various species is concerned. Risks should never be taken. In this context, the old adage 'It is better to be safe than sorry' should be borne in mind.

There are a very few species, such as Cockatiels, Ringneck Parakeets and lovebirds, which can be bred on the colony system, but the general rule for all other birds should be one pair per aviary.

By far the best method is to build aviaries in ranges. After preparing the site for a range, the ground should be covered with 13-mm. (½-in.) wire netting; this will exclude most vermin with the exception of mice.

Wire netting and welded mesh are obtainable in a large range of sizes and gauges. For lovebirds and the smaller parakeets, 25-mm. (1-in.) by 13-mm. (½-in.) welded mesh is the most suitable; although 1-in. by 1-in. is widely used for the larger birds, it does allow the entry of vermin such as young rats, stoats and weasels. After a tragic accident in which a rare parrot in my collection was killed by a predator, I have never recommended the use of welded mesh larger than 1-in. by ½-in. What happened was that a fox or some other predator frightened the bird at night so that if fell on to the aviary floor. As it climbed back up the wire to its perch, the predator caught hold of its leg, pulled it through the wire and bit its leg off at the top of the thigh. This would have been impossible if the smaller welded mesh had been used. I discovered afterwards that many aviculturists, especially those in rural areas, (although my own aviaries are in a built-up London suburb) have suffered similar losses.

Very large mesh 5-cm. (2-in.) square is sometimes used for the large macaws and cockatoos, but has the disadvantage of allowing the entry of such birds as sparrows, which will cause the seed bill to escalate. It also allows free access to a larger range of vermin and predators. If it is necessary to use large size welded mesh for birds which can destroy with ease any other type of wire, the only way to exclude sparrows and vermin is to double wire the aviary, with a wire of smaller mesh being placed in front of the heavy gauge wire.

All wire should be painted with black bitumen paint before use. This not only greatly prolongs the life of the wire but makes the occupants easier to observe and gives the aviary a neater appearance.

The wood used in aviary construction should be treated with a preservative. For destructive birds such as cockatoos and macaws metal piping should be used for the aviary framework. Wood has a short life in such aviaries and makes the danger of escape very real. It is natural for all parrots to gnaw, and the larger species can reduce wood to a pile of shavings in minutes if they so desire.

The wire netting or mesh should be stretched tightly across the frame as sagging spoils the appearance of the aviary. As aviaries are so expensive to build, and because it may be necessary to extend or move them, it is advisable to build them in sections.

It is *most* important to have two partitions of wire between adjoining aviaries to prevent the occupants being seriously injured by their neighbours. Newly fledged youngsters are especially vulnerable because some cling to the wire netting before they learn to perch. Very serious injuries, such as the removal of a mandible, can be inflicted through the wire.

It is advisable to build a fully enclosed shelter for each aviary, so that the occupants can be shut inside during severe weather. Many parrots can tolerate cold but cannot tolerate damp. If it is possible to shut them inside a fairly spacious shelter during damp winter weather, especially when it is foggy, they will fare much better.

It is a good idea to build the shelter slightly higher than the flight. A perch placed at the highest point, where it is out of draughts, will prove a cosy roosting place for those birds which do not use their nest-box for roosting. For those that do, the nest-box must be left in position throughout the year.

When designing a range of aviaries, there are many advantages to including a covered corridor along the back of the shelters. This prevents birds escaping, allows the owner to feed and tend the birds in dry and comfortable conditions and provides a place in which seed can be stored. Entrance into the flight should be via a door in the back of the shelter, not via a door in the flight. If this is done, a bird can escape only into the covered corridor.

The normal height of aviaries is 1.8m. (6-ft.) or to suit the height of the owner. Minimum width should be 76-cm. (2-ft. 6-in.) for small species such as lovebirds, Cockatiels and small parakeets, and 1.2-m. (4-ft.) or 1.8-m. (6-ft.) for large parrots, cockatoos and macaws. The length will depend on the space available and the species kept. For lovebirds, Cockatiels and grass parakeets, flights only 2.4-m. (8-ft.) long are quite suitable. Other parakeets and lorikeets require flights which are about 3.6-m. (12-ft.) in length and the larger parakeets, such as Pennants and Alexandrines, will appreciate flights which are up to 6-m. (20-ft.) long, although this length is by no means essential. The length of the flight is by far the most important dimension; the width is relatively unimportant for birds which spend much time flying.

Many birds will do well in indoor aviaries and will breed success- fully if the problem of low humidity can be overcome. The situation should be light and airy. Indoor aviaries have the advan- tage of electric lighting, which is most useful during the winter months. It can be installed with great benefit to the inhabitants in outdoor aviaries. The expense is well worthwhile. One of the hazards for parrots of winter in a temperate climate is the long night during which they cannot feed. This lowers their body temperature and their resistance to disease. Small species are especially vulnerable during the winter but even the largest parrots will benefit from artificial light. It will bring them into breeding condition earlier than birds kept under natural conditions, thus the hours of artificial light should be monitored to prevent them from nesting too early in the year.

Perches used in aviaries should be branches from deciduous trees such as elm and plane, and from fruit trees such as apple. They should be renewed regularly before they become smooth and slippery and because fresh branches provide parrots with great enjoyment. They love to remove the bark, twigs and leaves. Pet birds should be provided with twigs too; a daily supply offered to a caged parrot will help to keep it occupied and contented, and to prevent its beak from becoming overgrown.

Aviary floors can be of concrete, gravel, shingle or grass. Concrete is the most hygienic and the easiest to keep clean, especi- ally if it is laid to slope slightly towards the shelter; it can then be hosed down and the water swept out through the corridor.

Grass floors can look attractive and provide ground-feeding species with hours of enjoyment, as they eat the grass seeds and search for minerals. Unfortunately, they are a severe health risk for species such as Australian parakeets which usually harbour *Ascaridia* worms. While picking up items from the grass floor, the birds ingest the worm eggs excreted in the faeces and the chain of infection is started all over again. Thus grass floors cannot be recommended. On shingle floors the worm eggs are likely to work their way through the shingle and out of reach of the birds.

Aviaries should be cleaned regularly except when the birds are breeding. During this period they should be disturbed as little as possible. Some parrots will make it quite clear that intrusion is resented at this time by dive-bombing and even actually attacking anyone who dares to enter.

Every effort should be made to control mice; they carry disease and contaminate seed. It is impossible to prevent their entry and few aviaries are entirely free of these rodents which are attracted by the seed supply. It is possible to place traps inside an aviary if these are placed in small wooden boxes which have the front made of welded mesh, allowing access to mice only.

Great care must be taken when poison is used in the vicinity of aviaries; vermin could actually carry it inside an aviary.

Aviaries should always be sited so that they obtain as much protection from the elements as possible. Many parrots are inhabitants of dense tropical forest and do not appreciate strong sunlight. It is therefore a good idea to position aviaries near or under trees, which will provide some protection from the elements and a feeling of security, which an aviary in an open situation can never offer. This is very important for birds which are not naturally found in wide open spaces and could well be the reason why many captive parrots never attempt to breed. Australian parakeets and Cockatiels which are found naturally in open and semi-desert areas thrive in bare, open aviaries, but these conditions may well be detrimental to birds of dense forests. There are countless records of neotropical species and other canopy-dwelling parrots breeding in dark, secluded aviaries.

Birds in aviaries in exposed situations may need extra protection from the elements during the winter. It is a simple matter to make panels of clear plastic which can be fitted into position during cold weather to keep off prevailing winds.

Commercially manufactured parrot cages, the designs of which vary little, are available. They are expensive to purchase and it is difficult or impossible to obtain one suitable for the largest parrots and macaws. A welder could produce a superb cage for a pet parrot, far larger and less expensive than a manufactured one, so it is worthwhile making enquiries in this direction if a suitable cage cannot be found in a pet shop.

The cage obtained should be as large as the buyer can afford—certainly large enough to take two perches. One perch should be placed high up in the cage and it is this one on which the occupant will invariably choose to roost at night. If the cage contains only one perch, a suitable length of a tree branch should be cut. The thickness should be different from that of the perch provided, in order to give the bird's feet some exercise.

Most parrot cages are fitted with only two containers, one for food and the other for water. The size of the food container is often totally inadequate for a large parrot and would need to be refilled at least twice daily. It is therefore advisable to buy a strong metal hook-on container to use in addition. Unfortunately, some of the larger parrots will treat these as playthings and quickly learn to unhook them and throw them on the cage floor. Also, some birds resent the intrusion of a hand inside the cage to remove a food container, thus the inadequate feeding containers are a real drawback.

Some thought should be given to water containers for birds in aviaries. Receptacles for large parrots need to be heavy to prevent mischievous species from overturning them. They should also be relatively shallow for those which enjoy bathing. Some, like lories, are enthusiastic bathers and take a daily bath, no matter how cold the weather; others, including most cockatoos, bathe only in rain. Heavy earthenware dog bowls are suitable water containers for the larger birds and large white plastic drinkers, with two hooks, are ideal for the smaller species. Both types are obtainable from most pet stores.

No parrot can remain in good feather condition unless it has access to water; fulfil this easy requirement and most will remain in good condition with a glossy shine to the plumage.

Most parrot cages have a wire grid which is placed above the removable tray on the floor of the cage. This should be removed to allow the parrot to walk on the floor and to play there. Some of the smaller species like to lie on their back in play.

When buying a cage, attention should be paid to the door fastening. Virtually the only escape-proof type is the screw; an intelligent parrot will soon learn how to operate most other types!

The best floor covering for parrot cages is newspaper; occasionally one comes across a bird which will tear this up or carry it about, in which case sand or pet litter can be used. Newspaper should, of course, be changed daily.

Cages should be positioned out of draughts. They should not be placed in a window where there is no escape from strong sun, but most birds like to be near a window so that they can see what is going on outside.

A small parrot cage—the smallest size available—will be found most useful when it is necessary to catch a bird from an aviary to transfer it to another enclosure or to take it indoors, as it will be easier to take through an aviary door than a large cage.

Another essential piece of equipment is a catching net, without which it will be extremely difficult to catch a bird in an aviary. Such nets, in various sizes, can be obtained from aviary supply companies. Those made of nylon should be avoided as a small bird could catch its nails in the material and the struggle to free itself will cause additional stress to it.

Parrots moult once a year; those bred in the Northern Hemisphere and those which have been in captivity long enough to become thoroughly established, usually moult after the breeding season, that is between July and September. Certainly in the larger birds, not all the primaries are moulted in one year, thus it could be two or three years before a parrot which has had its flight feathers cut renews each one.

Finally, on the subject of cages and their contents, a pet bird should never be without something on which it can occupy its beak or with which to amuse itself. Small playful birds, such as conures, will appreciate toys similar to those manufactured for budgerigars. The larger parrots are capable of destroying anything made from plastic and should therefore be provided with lumps of wood or large nuts which they cannot open but which will, nevertheless, occupy them for hours.

Feeding

A popular misconception which needs to be refuted before the dietary requirements of parrots can be understood is that these birds are seed-eaters by nature. This is true of the species which are most readily kept and bred in captivity—and this is the very reason why they are so successful under captive conditions. Budgerigars and other Australian parakeets, Cockatiels and, to a lesser degree, lovebirds, feed principally on seeds in the wild. Unfortunately, a similar diet came to be applied to all members of the parrot family which are commonly kept in captivity, although some would never, or rarely, feed on seeds in their natural habitat. Generally speaking, parrots are omnivorous; their natural diet is a varied one—and so it should be in captivity.

Seed will form the basis of the diet for most species, with the exception of certain specialised feeders such as lories. The owner of one or two pet birds usually buys 'parrot mixture' in packets. This consists of about 90 per cent sunflower seed, with the addition of a few peanuts and chillies and perhaps also hard maize and a few oats. This can be supplemented with seeds bought by the pound from bird seed suppliers. I would suggest that a pound each of pine nuts (for the larger species), hemp, white millet and canary seed is bought and each seed offered in a separate container to discover the preferences of pet birds. The favoured seeds can then be added to the staple seed mixture.

Where more than a few birds are kept, it is uneconomical to buy seed in packets, partly because seed is far cheaper when bought in quantity and partly because when mixtures are fed much seed is wasted, because the birds discard those they do not like. For this reason, each kind of seed should be provided in a separate container. Also, if mixtures containing unwanted seeds are offered, it may appear to the owner who is not familiar with a bird's preferences that the bird has plenty of food before it when it may be almost starving. Many parrots will steadfastly refuse certain seeds and there is little point in persevering with these beyond a reasonable trial period.

As a guide, it is suggested that the smaller species—lovebirds, Cockatiels, parakeets, etc.—are offered canary seed, white and panicum millet, niger, hemp and sunflower seed and that the larger birds are offered sunflower, pine nuts, peanuts and canary seed and white millet. Millet sprays and oats can be offered to both groups.

It should be pointed out for those with no previous experience of keeping birds that they must *always* have food available. Of non-perishable foods, such as seeds, they should be provided daily with slightly more than they can eat in a day. Perishable foods, such as fruits, vegetables, bread and milk should be offered in small quantities, which will be consumed immediately. If it is possible, it is better to provide such foods two or three times daily than to feed them once in larger quantities. It also makes life more interesting for the birds; the large species especially will eagerly await the feeding of these items.

It should not be forgotten that, unlike many birds, parrots and again, especially the larger species, have a very keen sense of taste and therefore really appreciate a varied diet. In any case, this is essential because most seeds are deficient in essential constituents. Many parrots which are fed entirely on seed, either because other items are refused or not offered, suffer from vitamin deficiencies which affect their health and, ultimately, their life-span. This is quite unnecessary, for such deficiences are easily corrected by adding a multivitamin preparation to the drinking water. The fruit flavoured ones made for children are particularly good as some birds will refuse drinking water to which have been added vitamin drops with an unpleasant taste.

However, birds which readily eat greenfoods and fruit are unlikely to suffer from such deficiencies. It is believed that birds do not require Vitamin C but they do need Vitamins A and B. Raw carrot is an excellent source of Vitamin A and an attempt should be made to persuade all parrots to eat it. Some parrots, especially Eclectus and certain South American species, have a great need for Vitamin A. In Eclectus Parrots, a deficiency results in monilliasis, which manifests itself in the form of a swelling in the mouth, often just under the tongue. Any parrot which suddenly ceases to eat seed should be examined for a swelling involving the lower jaw. If one is found the bird must immediately be taken to a veterinary surgeon for treatment.

Vitamins of the B complex are the ones most likely to be deficient in parrots. One of the most important is Vitamin B_2 (riboflavin). It is necessary for the enzyme system which enables the body cells to metabolise food energy. Brewer's yeast is the richest source. Alternatively, a yeast mixture specially prepared for birds can be obtained at any pet shop; its regular use, sprinkled on seed, will prove most beneficial.

A major source of the required vitamins are fresh vegetables and green leaves. These can include spinach beet (the leaves only, or the whole plant when it is seeding), lettuce, lucerne and such weeds as seeding grasses, chickweed, sowthistle, dandelion (leaves or the whole plant) and dock. Care must be taken when gathering wild foods that they have not been sprayed with a toxic substance.

Vegetables which can be offered, in addition to carrot, include celery, peas in the pod and—considered a great delicacy by the larger birds—corn-on-the-cob. Leaves and stalks of cabbage and cauliflower can be offered but are seldom eaten with the enthusiasm shown for the other foods mentioned.

The owner of one or two pet birds, even although he has no garden or allotment, could grow enough spinach beet in a window box to provide a daily supply of a few leaves throughout the year.

Berries are a superb food and they form a large part of the natural diet of many species. The berries of hawthorn and elder are great favourites with many birds.

A wild food which is relished by lovebirds and will be eaten by some parakeets is pussy willow or sallow. Lovebirds will eat the buds, bark, leaves, stalk and even the catkins.

Fruit helps to add variety to a parrot's diet and contains various mineral elements. Apple is widely fed; oranges, pears, tangerines and grapes can also be offered. Various fruits in season, especially pomegranates and cherries, also soft fruits such as redcurrants, blackberries and raspberries can be supplied. The food value of banana is far higher than that of most fruits but many birds will not sample it. Dried fruits, such as figs, dates and sultanas which have been soaked, will be relished by some birds.

Most people are aware that many small birds, such as tits, become almost totally insectivorous while rearing young. This is because protein is necessary for the growth of their chicks. Parrots must also have protein foods while rearing young. The traditional way of providing it is bread and milk; this is an excellent food but unfortunately not all birds will take it. Finding an acceptable substitute is therefore very much a question of trial and error, as parrots are highly individual in their food preferences. Items which can be tried include tinned strained meals prepared for human babies, proprietary Canary rearing food and soaked wholemeal bread mixed with hard boiled egg. Foods prepared for other live-stock, such as lucerne nuts, are also suitable; these have a high protein content. In the U.S.A., the various chows, such as trout chow and dog chow, are widely used by breeders of parrots and other birds. Bread and milk can also be supplemented and I do this by adding wheatgerm cereal to the milk before the bread is added, then sprinkle a small amount of a vitamin/mineral powder over it.

Milk has the added advantage of containing calcium. Rickets, caused through a lack of calcium, is regrettably common in the larger parrot species. Affected birds may leave the nest with feet which are almost useless; they therefore have to be destroyed. If milk is refused by the parents, calcium lactate tablets should be crushed and the resulting powder sprinkled over the rearing foods. Cheese is another excellent source of calcium and a food which is relished by many of the larger parrots. Leafy vegetables also contain calcium. It is vital for laying hens and is best provided in the form of cuttlefish bone. If it is not provided, the bird has to draw on the resources of its own body and calcium will be taken in excess from the bones, sometimes resulting in paralysis. Breeders will notice the hugely increased intake of cuttlefish bone in laying hens and in those which are rearing young.

Grit should also be available although some birds will ignore it. The smaller species can be given grit which is prepared for budgerigars; the larger species should be offered pigeon grit. Some parrots in aviaries will pick it up if sprinkled on the aviary floor, yet ignore it if it is provided in a container. Grit, which is only essential for seed-eating birds, is used in the gizzard to grind up seed.

A question often asked is whether or not table scraps are harmful to pet birds. Generally speaking they are not—if given in moderation. Meat is excellent and the larger parrots enjoy nothing more than a chop bone. Cooked vegetables, plain cake, biscuits and toast crusts can safely be offered. Bread need never be wasted in a house where there are several parrots. Cut up into small pieces and baked in the oven until crisp, it will be greatly enjoyed. And bread and milk can be given to birds whether or not they are breeding.

A point which deserves to be stressed is that some newly

imported birds are unfamiliar with seed and could starve to death if this fact is not realised. In some quarantine stations seed is not offered, thus the birds will have to be gradually weaned on to seed from a diet of soft foods, such as boiled maize or turkey starter mash. One way to do this is to mix soaked sunflower seed with the soft food offered, then gradually mix dry sunflower with the soaked seed and reduce the amount of soft food fed.

Soaked and sprouted seeds are more beneficial and easier to digest than dry seed; if the choice of dry or soaked seed is offered to parrots which are rearing young, they usually take the soaked seed exclusively. Sunflower can be soaked in water for 24 hours, then washed thoroughly and left in a warm place for another 24 hours, by which time it will have started to sprout. Canary seed can also be fed soaked.

Hooded Parakeet

Breeding

Nothing in the aviculturist's world produces as much satisfaction as the sight of newly fledged young in his aviaries. The sight could represent the culmination of several year's hopes in the case of some pairs—for there is so much that can go wrong. It is as well not to be too optimistic when breeding parrots for, unless blessed with extraordinary good fortune, the disappointments will outnumber the successes.

It has already been explained that the major requirement for each breeding pair is an aviary to themselves, and for this reason starting off with parrots is more expensive than keeping such birds as finches. A collection of several pairs of the latter can be kept in an aviary which could contain only one pair of parakeets, thus anyone with limited space at their disposal should bear this point in mind.

When housing breeding pairs, similar or closely-related species should not be placed in adjoining aviaries. If this is done, the males may spend the whole breeding season attempting to get at their rivals next door, with the result that they are too busy to fertilise the female's eggs. Thus pairs of grass parakeets, for example, should be separated by pairs of Rosellas or Cockatiels. There is, however, an advantage in having two pairs of the same or of a closely-related species, because in the event of a hen being unable or unwilling to tend her young, it is often possible to transfer them to the nest of another female.

In the Northern Hemisphere, parakeets will come into breeding condition during March or April, with the exception of the *Psittacula* parakeets, such as Ringnecks, which are early breeders. Their nest-boxes should be in position by the beginning of February, but for most other parrots March will be early enough.

Birds such as lories, lovebirds and conures which roost in their nest-boxes should have access to them all the year round. Most breeders of the large birds such as cockatoos, macaws and the larger parrots, also leave their boxes in position throughout the year, although the birds do not normally roost inside.

A suitable nest-box can make all the difference between failure and success, for some birds will make no attempt to nest unless everything about the site is exactly to their liking. It has often been found that moving the position of a nest-box or turning the entrance to face in another direction has had the almost immediate effect of the female entering, whereas before she had shown no interest in the box or log.

Natural logs are particularly desirable to birds, and allowing them to excavate the interior often stimulates a female parrot to breed. The problem with logs is that they are very difficult to inspect, unless modified in some way.

A common mistake is to provide a box or log which is too large for the species. It should not be forgotten that in the wild suitable nesting holes are not always easy for parrots to find and that, especially in the case of the large species, large holes would seldom be available. If a hen is offered a choice of nesting sites, all other factors being equal, she will usually choose the smallest. This certainly provides a greater sense of security. An entrance hole which is only just large enough for the bird to squeeze into will be appreciated for the same reason. However, the depth of the box is important because if it is too shallow, the young could leave the nest prematurely.

The high cost of wood means that nest-boxes, especially for the larger species, are expensive to build. Parrots have a great need to gnaw, a need which is most evident when they come into breeding condition, for in the wild they would be preparing the nest. In a couple of seasons a female may gnaw right through the side or base of her nest-box. Costly and inconvenient repairs can be avoided by nailing pieces of wood to the inside of the nest; these can be oddments left over from the construction of aviaries or nest-boxes.

Planks of timber or heavy-grade plywood are suitable for nest-box construction. An upright oblong is the usual design and will suit most birds. Most fanciers make a round entrance hole in the middle of the box near the top. A quicker and easier method and one which is just as acceptable to the birds is to cut a square out of one corner before the box is assembled. There is also an advantage from the birds' point of view. The interior of the nest will be unevenly lit, so that the occupants can use the corner of the box which is most to their liking. A nest which admits too much light will not be used.

Below the entrance hole some narrow strips of wood or even staples must be fixed so that access to the bottom of the nest is easy and also allows the young to find their way out. Wire netting is sometimes recommended for this purpose, but as many breeders know to their cost, there is a danger of a bird's nail becoming hooked up in the wire, possibly with fatal results.

Small nest-boxes should be attached by means of a strong screw attached to the side of the aviary which fits into a hole in the back of the box near the top. If it is permanently screwed to a wooden support, it will be difficult to take the box down quickly in an emergency.

Many breeding failures could be averted if the nest-box was easily accessible for inspection. Some hens leave the nest so rarely or cover the young so closely that it is impossible to follow their progress. All this can be rectified by placing the nest-box on the outside of the aviary. However, this is not without its dangers, especially if nest-boxes are liable to interference from children, in which case a safety box would have to be placed over the nest, if necessary with a lock on it. When nest-boxes are fitted to the outside of the aviary it is a simple matter to carry out inspection when the female is in the aviary and she will not be aware of the fact.

It is even possible to give the young supplementary feeds if the parents are not feeding them adequately, which is a great advantage for many aviculturists who are not able to remove young for hand-rearing. With the aid of a syringe from which the needle has been removed, chicks can be fed very quickly in the nest, using a mixture of milk, baby cereal and bone meal.

To return to the subject of nest-boxes, although a removable lid is a convenient means of inspecting a small nest-box, some birds will panic if inspection takes place from above because they have to move upwards to reach the exit. An inspection door in one side, a few inches above the level of the nest, allowing for nesting material, in some cases is therefore preferable. In a tall nest-box this is essential because the breeder will not be able to reach the nest proper without taking the box down.

Some birds resent nest inspection; others do not. In nervous birds or those which are so vicious when in breeding condition that it is not possible to enter the aviary, nest inspection will be impossible unless the nest-box is placed on the outside of the aviary.

Some birds will not accept any kind of nest filling and will throw out any kind provided. Others will provide their own by gnawing small splinters of wood from the inside of the box, sometimes to a depth of 3-cm. (1-in.) or more.

It is often asked whether the nest-box should be hung in the flight or in the shelter. There are advantages to both locations, although most breeders of parakeets and lovebirds place the nest-box in the flight. I believe it is a good idea to provide a box in each place, as some hens will prefer the privacy offered by a box in the shelter. The disadvantage of this site is that it will not have the benefit of rain, which provides the necessary humidity. However, if one nest fails for this reason, the nest-box can be transferred to the outside flight. The main disadvantages of this location are that the birds will be more subject to disturbance from outside sources and that, in very hot weather, the female and the young could suffer. In this case, overhead shade should be provided, preferably before the birds start to nest.

Species which come from areas of dense forest will prefer shady or dark locations in which to nest, while those from wide open spaces, such as most Australian parakeets, might even refuse to nest if there are trees overhanging the nest-box. Their instinct is to avoid such sites which would offer little protection from predators such as snakes.

Pairs should be provided with the same nest, year after year, as some hens may take a long time to become accustomed to a new nest-box. This is less likely to apply in the case of birds such as lories and conures which use their nest-boxes throughout the year for roosting. In practice, many of these birds will enter a new nest within minutes, or even seconds, of it being placed in the aviary, for they are so inquisitive.

In the wild, not all parrots use holes in trees as nesting sites. Some use termites' nests or even caves in rocks, while some small species, such as parrotlets, will even nest in fence posts and lovebirds in holes in dwelling houses. However, in captivity all parrots will use nest-boxes.

The breeder will be aware that his birds are taking an interest in nesting when they start to examine the nest and when courtship display and feeding are seen. Courtship display is not well defined in the majority of parrots; in many it consists of little more than strutting up and down with the tail flared and the pupils of the eyes dilated. It is more pronounced in the parrots from the Old World. Typical courtship behaviour in the male Princess of Wales' Parakeet, for example, starts with short flights around the female, bowing as he alights. The head feathers are fluffed and the contour feathers are drawn tightly to the body, the wings being partly spread. He then races to and fro, chattering constantly. In Rosella parakeets, the male fluffs up the feathers of the breast and the upper tail coverts, moves his fanned tail from side to side and either bows or holds the head high and tilts it back, at the same time drooping the wings.

The female normally lays her eggs on alternate days, although it is not unusual for there to be two whole days between egg laying. In the larger parrots, the interval between eggs can be three or four days.

Incubation starts when the first or second egg is laid. This means that the ages of the chicks in one nest vary and there could be a difference in age as great as two weeks between the oldest and the youngest. In such a case the youngest chick would not stand a very good chance of survival.

All parrots' eggs are white, as is normal in hole-nesting birds. The shape varies and can differ even among the eggs which form one clutch.

The shortest incubation periods are those of the Australian parakeets whose eggs hatch in 18 days (in the budgerigar) or 19 to 20 days (other species). For most true parrots the incubation period is 26 to 28 days, and in the large cockatoos incubation can exceed 32 days for each egg.

The number of eggs laid varies not only among the different genera of parrots but according to their geographical distribution; birds inhabiting areas near the Equator often lay small clutches and breed more than once during the year, for food is continually abundant. Those which lay large clutches may be taking advantage of a seasonal food supply, such as seeding grasses. Also, small clutch size is related to a longer incubation period, and vice versa.

In all parrots the female is fed on food regurgitated by the male while she is incubating and during the early part of the chicks' lives or for most of the time that they remain in the nest. Some males will enter the nest and feed the chicks; others never do.

The importance of providing nutritious foods while the young are being reared cannot be over-emphasised. Information on this point is given in the section on feeding.

Some young parrots will be seen looking out of the nest for

Moustache Parakeet

Splendid Parakeet

several days, or even weeks, before they actually leave it. Those that do are generally more steady on leaving the nest, for they have had plenty of time to view the outside world. Some young birds are extremely nervous when they fledge.

Most will be feeding themselves within two weeks but they should be watched very carefully to ensure that they are fully independent before they are removed from their parents.

From the time the eggs are laid up to the day the young birds are removed from their parents there is a great deal that can go wrong. One of the most common problems is dead-in-shell, that is, chicks which die in the egg, usually just before hatching. It is impossible to be dogmatic about the cause, as a lot is still to be learnt on this point. Sometimes the chicks fail to penetrate the shell because it is too hard. A dry atmosphere is often blamed, thus with hens which allow nest inspection, it can do no harm to sprinkle the eggs lightly with warm water. Other reasons given for dead-in-shell are dietary deficiencies and breeding from closely-related birds.

Infertile eggs are common among young birds, especially of the larger species. Occasionally one comes across a hen which will enter the nest-box as soon as it is placed in position and which comes out so rarely that the male does not have an opportunity to mate with her. In such cases the nest entrance should be nailed up. The larger birds will gnaw the cover away in a few days, but it must be removed after about a week for the smaller birds.

Birds of both sexes may eat or break the eggs soon after they are laid. If a bird is known to have this habit, it should be provided with a specially constructed nest-box with a false bottom containing sawdust or peat. A concave base to the nest with a hole in the centre, just large enough for the egg to pass through when it is laid, will allow the eggs to be collected and placed under a more reliable female or in an incubator.

Probably the most frequent mistake of beginners is one caused through impatience! As soon as it is thought that the eggs are overdue, they open them, only to find to their mortification that in so doing they have killed a living chick. Nothing is to be gained from opening eggs—and everything can be lost. One seldom knows precisely when a female starts to incubate as this does not always occur with the laying of the first or second egg; also, cold weather can prolong the incubation period. It is therefore the wise aviculturist who allows the female to sit for two weeks past the calculated hatching time. Then—and only then—should the eggs be removed.

On holding them up to a strong light it will be possible to ascertain if they are fertile. An infertile egg is light in weight, colour and appearance and is therefore known as 'clear'. A fertile egg is heavier, looks dull and, when held up to the light, appears solid.

It is a wise breeder who arms himself in advance of any problems occurring with a small incubator, because sooner or later it is certain to be required. Even if, at the time, there is no other hen available to take the eggs, they can be placed in an incubator for a few days or kept there for the remainder of the incubation period. It is difficult, but not impossible, to hand-rear chicks from the egg but much easier to start them off under another parrot, preferably a hen which has proved reliable as a foster and, if she already has chicks, one which is of a closely-related species.

The temperature of the incubator should be set at 100 deg. F. (33 deg. C.) and the eggs should be turned twice daily. Humidity is essential and the water container must be kept filled.

When the chicks hatch, they can be transferred to the nest of an incubating hen of a less valued species if her eggs are due to hatch in the fairly near future. However, hens have been known to feed fostered chicks even if they have been setting for only a few days. Of course, if a hen with very young chicks is available, the breeder need not resort to this.

Hand-rearing from the egg is not a task for someone with no previous experience of hand-feeding parrot chicks. This is a much easier task when attempted with chicks which are a few days old. They need to be kept in a temperature of 92 deg. F. (33 deg. C.), and should be placed in a small cardboard box inside an incubator, heated cage or hospital cage. In an emergency, a warm airing cupboard might suffice. They can be placed on a bed of paper tissues.

Hand-rearing is time consuming, but it is also extremely rewarding and instructive, resulting in a real insight into the development of a parrot chick. When a few days old, it will need to be fed about every two hours. I feed chicks between 6 a.m. and 11 p.m. During their first night away from their parents, I feed them at 3 a.m., but otherwise they are left throughout the night.

A fairly thin mixture of milk and baby cereal will prove satisfactory for most chicks. This can be fed by means of an eye-dropper for newly hatched chicks or by using a syringe which has had the needle removed, or a teaspoon for slightly older chicks. The teaspoon should be modified by bending the sides inwards so that its shape is not unlike that of the parents' lower mandible.

Eye-dropper or syringe should be warmed slightly before feeding or the food will be refused. The teaspoon can be warmed by using it to stir the food, which must, of course, be heated before feeding. To ensure that chicks receive adequate calcium, the powder from scraping cuttlefish bone or bone meal should be added to the food.

It is extremely important to examine the crop of each chick before each feed. If food remains in the crop well after a period when it would normally be empty, action must be taken. The chick should be fed molasses diluted in hot water and, if possible, the crop should be gently massaged. In extreme cases, it may be necessary to remove the crop contents using a tube. However, it is seldom that either action will be necessary. To wean chicks on to seed, they should be offered soaked seed, also soft fruits.

Hand-rearing is condemned by some fanciers who believe that hand-reared birds will be incapable of rearing their own young. This is quite untrue. It has been proved on many occasions that hand-reared birds are satisfactory parents; indeed, they are often superior to parent-reared birds, because they have little fear of people, thus nest inspection does not cause them any stress.

By the same token, it has often been stated that former pet birds are of no use for breeding. Again this is quite untrue. Such birds are often excellent parents and nest more readily than wild caught birds of the same species because, being tame, they are under less stress.

Care of Sick Birds

No one should contemplate keeping birds unless they are able to devote part of every day to caring for them. Although one can buy seed hoppers which contain enough food to last a bird several days, I feel that their use is to be discouraged. Daily attention to a bird's needs is essential, otherwise the fact that a bird is unwell could pass unnoticed.

The course of an illness is usually very swift—a bird which looks only slightly unwell one day may be dead the next. Countless deaths could be averted if the owner took action immediately. The first question that a beginner will ask in this context is how to recognise a sick bird? The observant owner will be able to do this quickly and this is why it is so important to know each bird as an individual.

A healthy bird normally rests on one foot when it has its head tucked into the feathers of the back. When I pass an aviary and see a bird resting thus, I automatically check to see how many feet it is resting on. Young birds rest on two feet as a matter of course and occasionally one sees an adult which is perfectly fit sitting in this way. But this is often the first clue that alerts the owner to the fact that something is wrong.

Having seen an adult bird resting on two feet, with the head tucked into the feathers of the back, the next step is to check its eyes and droppings. A bird which has eyes which look dull and *sunken* is definitely sick. If on being disturbed it immediately tucks its head into its back, this is further proof that it is unwell. The condition of its droppings will be a pointer to someone who knows the bird and its feeding habits. It has been stated so often that a parrot which has green and loose droppings is unwell that, on countless occasions, parrot owners have told me that they do not give their birds fruit because this makes the droppings loose. This is nothing to worry about. Also, the droppings of many of the larger parrots are naturally green—especially Amazons, macaws, etc. Thus droppings are only a guide to the health of a bird if one knows what their condition is normally. The important signs to look for are droppings which are extremely watery and mainly white. The white part of the faeces is the urine, thus when produced on its own it may be an indication of kidney disorder. I do not hesitate to bring a parrot indoors during a severe winter if it is suffering from the cold and have often noticed that such birds have very watery droppings.

The first and most vital requirement of a sick bird is heat. This cannot be over-emphasised. Heat alone will often be effective in saving an ailing bird. Most beginners make the mistake of not providing a high enough temperature, 85 to 90 deg. F. (29 to 32 deg. C.) being required. In my opinion, easily the best way of providing this is by an infra-red lamp. For many reasons this is infinitely superior to a hospital cage. This is especially true for a pet bird, for it will not be necessary to move it from the cage in which it lives. Additionally, if the lamp is directed to one side of the cage, the bird can move out of the heat if and when it so desires.

The specially manufactured hospital cages may prove satisfactory for some birds, but I cannot recommend their use for parrots. The interior is completely lacking in humidity and this does not suit these birds. I would advise the owner of even a single pet parrot to invest in an infra-red lamp, which will cost only a very small proportion of the cost of the bird and could well be the means of saving its life.

A sick bird should be placed in a quiet place and immediately given the benefit of the heat of an infra-red lamp. The bird's food should not be in the heat of the lamp, which should be placed about 20-cm. (8-in.) from the cage. No harmful effects will result in leaving the lamp on for several days, if necessary.

The next step is to seek professional advice. There are many diseases from which a bird can suffer but the symptons hardly vary so it will usually be impossible to correctly diagnose the illness. It is for this reason that most veterinary surgeons will prescribe a broad spectrum antibiotic which will cure some of the more usual illnesses. A bird which has been subjected to the warmth of an infra-red lamp should not be taken to a veterinary surgeon's surgery as the change in temperature and location will quickly affect it adversely. A bird which is suffering from an injury rather than an illness can, of course, be attended to on a veterinary surgeon's premises, but if it is suffering from shock it, too, will need heat and must be kept warm. On a car journey, for example, a blanket must be kept around the cage.

Antibiotics can be given in powder or suspension (liquid) or, in the case of large birds which are less likely to suffer the effects of shock, they can be injected into the bird. If the antibiotic is to be placed in the bird's drinking water, fruit or other foods on which it could quench its thirst should be withheld. Alternatively, the antibiotic can be placed on a favourite item of food—inside a grape for example.

Some sick birds stop feeding, in which case it may be necessary for a veterinary surgeon to dose the bird using a syringe with a tube on the end. The tube is placed in the bird's mouth and gently pushed down the throat so that the liquid is directed at once into the bird's crop.

Sick birds which stop eating hard foods such as seed must be tempted to eat with almost any item of soft food. For instance, a nutritious mixture can be made up of baby cereal, milk and mashed banana or sugar which a sick bird might take readily, its normal foods remaining untouched. It is essential to experiment in such cases. Any nutritious foods can be tried before the bird becomes so weak that it loses all interest in food.

If it recovers, the daily addition of a drop of a multi-vitamin preparation to the drinking water each day will be beneficial. Several common diseases in parrots are caused by vitamin deficiencies; also, birds which have been treated with antibiotics have a greater need for vitamins.

On recovery, the high temperature in which a sick bird has been kept must be gradually lowered until the heat is dispensed with. A bird which has come from an outdoor aviary should not be returned in cold weather and this can mean keeping it indoors for some weeks.

During the breeding season, a watch should be kept for egg-bound hens. Fortunately, a bird which is unable to lay an egg usually leaves the nest-box and will be seen sitting huddled and dejected in the aviary or on the floor. Immediate heat is required and, here again, an infra-red lamp will prove invaluable. Normally heat alone enables the female to pass her egg.

What makes a bird ill? Those in aviaries can be infected by wild birds or mice which are carrying disease, or they can pick up stale or mouldy food from the aviary floor. A dusty atmosphere or dusty seed can cause the fungus disease aspergillosis, for example, for which there is no cure which is universally available. Thus cleanliness is important, but it is not possible to carry it to extremes, especially during the breeding season when it will be unwise or impossible to enter certain aviaries.

Seed and water containers must be kept clean and drinking water should be changed daily, in cages and aviaries.

While on the subject of health, mention should be made of the virus disease ornithosis, which is known as psittacosis in parrots. It is seldom found in aviary-bred parrots, being most likely to occur in newly imported birds.

The national press has devoted many a sensational headline to this disease which, in the past, was known to have proved fatal to human beings in some cases. However, these days it is easily cured with the use of antibiotics. It is difficult to describe the symptons in a parrot because these are so similar to a number of other diseases. In human beings the symptons are such that the affected person will probably believe that he or she has influenza; however, there is no cold or cough. An affected person will have a high temperature and be feverish, alternately shivering and hot and will perspire heavily during the night. The body will ache and after a few days without treatment the lungs will be affected, making breathing difficult after any exertion, such as walking upstairs. Recovery will be rapid after antibiotics have been taken, thus a doctor should be consulted immediately psittacosis is suspected.

Australian Cockatiel

Cockatiels

The Cockatiel is the bird which introduces many fanciers to the parrot family—and a more suitable species with which to start could not be chosen. It is a totally delightful bird, equally at home indoors or out, in cage or aviary. As a pet it has no equal among parrots of the same size.

It has every virtue for which the aviculturist could wish. It breeds readily and various colour mutations have been established; it is extremely long-lived and very hardy; it is always steady, if not tame and, most important for the breeder, adult birds can be sexed at a glance. Add to this its pleasing personality and the simplicity with which it can be cared for, and it is easy to see why the Cockatiel is so popular.

In the U.S.A. it is widely kept as a pet but, for some reason, has never attained the same degree of popularity as in Europe. Clearly it needs a public relations officer!

The colour of the wild Cockatiel is mainly grey. The male has a broad white patch extending the length of the wing, and a vivid orange patch on the cheeks surrounded by an area of white, the rest of the head and part of the crest being yellow. The underside of the tail is black. The beak is grey. Females and young birds of both sexes have a much smaller area of yellow on the head, the orange cheek patches are less vivid and the crest is dull yellow and grey. The underside of the tail is barred with yellow and grey to form a most attractive pattern. Cockatiels measure about 32-cm. (12-in.).

It is essential to buy a young bird if it is to be kept as a pet. It will be most easily tamed if obtained as soon as it is independent, that is one to two weeks after leaving the nest. In order to purchase such a young bird, it is necessary to buy from the breeder. In the Northern Hemisphere Cockatiels start to breed during March or April, thus young birds will be available between April and September.

Some breeders hand-rear youngsters, which are then completely tame and fearless. Such birds will, of course, cost considerably more than one which has been reared by its parents. However, if one of the latter is obtained at an early age, it will become equally as tame as a hand-reared bird, whereas one which is several months old may never become completely tame.

When they are young, it is impossible to distinguish the sex of these birds with certainty. However, this hardly matters as both sexes make good pets, although possibly males learn to talk more readily. The 'talking' voice of a Cockatiel is quiet and rather squeaky. Some birds are quick to learn and will acquire their first phrase after a few weeks. A simple phrase, such as 'come on' or 'hello' should be chosen to start with, and another should not be repeated until the first has been learned. The more time that is spent with a bird which is being taught to mimic, whether it is a Cockatiel or one of the larger parrots, the sooner it is likely to learn each phrase.

Taming should be a gradual process. For the first few days, or for several weeks in the case of a nervous bird, no physical effort should be made to tame it. At first, it is most important to talk quietly to it often and to place its cage in a position where it will constantly have company and attention.

When it has thoroughly settled down an attempt should be made to train the Cockatiel to step on to one's finger. This is done by placing the hand inside the cage and gently pressing the forefinger against the bird's abdomen, just above the feet. After this has been carried out a few times, the bird will usually learn to step on to the hand. Some of the larger parrots will learn to do this but many will not and, in fact, show a fear of hands although they are quite tame in other respects.

When a Cockatiel has learned to step on to its owner's hand it can be allowed out of its cage. This should be done by leaving the cage door open and allowing the bird to find its own way out. If allowed to come out in its own time it is more likely to find its way back on its own. However, if it is slow to learn this it can be persuaded to step on to the finger and carried back to its cage.

It might be rather nervous after its first outing and refuse to step on to the offered finger. In this case the curtains should be closed (to prevent the bird flying at speed into the glass) and it should be gently picked up and returned to the cage. Larger parrots which can inflict painful bites should be picked up in a folded towel.

Young Cockatiels quickly become tame. They are inquisitive and mischievous and will delight in spending much time perched on a member of the household. The more freedom they are allowed, the tamer they will become. A tame Cockatiel will become part of the family and, with luck, will live for many years. It is not exceptional for these birds to live for more than 20 years. I have a pair which are well into their twenties and the cock is as active as a two year old and in perfect feather. The female is a little bald on the head—but that did not stop her laying when she was over 20 years old.

Cockatiels usually remain in excellent health on a mainly seed diet. They are extremely easy to care for. The staple diet should consist of white and panicum millet, canary seed and niger. Some birds will eat sunflower seed and all will relish spray millet. Apple and various greenfoods should also be offered. When rearing young, bread and milk should be available. If sunflower seed is offered at this time, it should be soaked or sprouted.

There are few cages on the market which are truly suitable for a pet Cockatiel. If the bird spends much time outside its cage, the size is less important. But if it is to be let out only for short periods, some thought should be given to providing the most suitable type of cage. This should not be an orthodox parrot cage because Cockatiels are active birds which need to move from perch to perch. For this reason a cage which is longer than it is tall is desirable.

As Cockatiels are not usually destructive birds, a wooden cage can be used. Suggested size is 90-cm. (3-ft.) long and about 25-cm. (10-in.) deep and tall. The larger pet shops can provide wire cage fronts, complete with door, with which to make a 'box cage'. The back, sides and top should be enclosed and can be made of wood or some easily cleaned material such as formica. A space must be left beneath the bottom of the wire front and the cage floor for a sliding tray.

Cockatiels spend much time in mutual preening of the head, thus a tame Cockatiel will greatly appreciate having its head scratched. When a young bird is being finger-tamed, one can also move the finger slowly towards the head and very gently scratch behind the crest. Few Cockatiels can resist this attention.

The great enjoyment to be obtained from a pet Cockatiel may instil a desire to breed these birds. As they breed more readily in captivity than most parrots, success is more likely to be achieved than with most species. But it is seldom that problems are not encountered—and this applies whichever species is chosen.

Where space is limited and available only indoors, Cockatiels are a good choice because they do not need large cages. However, a breeding cage for a pair should be at least 1.2m. (4-ft.) long; if the cage is indoors the nest-box can be attached to the outside, so that nest inspection can be carried out without causing any disturbance. The exact dimensions of the box are not important, but should be in the region of 20-cm. (8-in.) square and 30-cm. (12-in.) high. The entrance hole near the top of the box should be about 6-cm. (2½-in.) in diameter.

Cockatiels should be fully mature before they are allowed to breed, that is not before they are 10 or 11 months old. However, it is best to pair a bird which has not nested before with one which has, as the combination of experience and youth is more likely to prove successful than that of two inexperienced birds.

In Cockatiels the incubation period is shared, the male incubating during the day and the female during the night. The number of eggs in a clutch is usually above five, but on occasions a female will lay a very large clutch, so large in fact that proper incubation is impossible. In this case it is advisable to leave the pair with only six eggs to incubate, removing those laid last. It will be very difficult for them to cover more than this number properly, with the result that they fail to hatch. Incubation usually starts with the laying of the first or second egg, thus if a large number of eggs are left in the nest and some do hatch, there could be such a large discrepancy between the ages of the eldest and the youngest chicks that the youngest stand little chance of survival.

Incubation will be easier for the birds if the nest-box is fitted with a concave bottom, similar to those sold in pet shops for budgerigar nest-boxes. Some birds will gnaw the inside of the box to make a few slivers of wood on which to rest the eggs; if they do not, a handful of sawdust will prove useful in absorbing the moisture in the chicks' faeces. Where several chicks are being reared, the provision of a little sawdust every few days will help to keep the nest in a sanitary condition.

The incubation period is 19 days but could be extended in cold weather. When the chicks hatch they have an abundant covering of yellow down. They will be brooded and fed by both parents. Inexperienced birds sometimes allow their first chicks to die but, if this happens, disappointment should not be too great as they will usually feed the chicks of the next clutch quite satisfactorily. However, if the chicks are consistently allowed to die, it is advisable to replace one of the pair with an experienced bird.

If it is possible to start off with two pairs of Cockatiels, losses can often be avoided by transferring chicks which are not being fed to the nest of the other hen. This is only possible if she has young of approximately the same age.

When chicks are about 10 days old the parents cease to brood them during part of the day. This is the danger period for, if the weather is cold, the chicks may become chilled, which will result in their death.

Young Cockatiels develop quickly and leave the nest when aged between four and five weeks old. On occasions, the female will have laid the first egg of the next clutch before the last young bird has left the nest. Cockatiels usually rear two nests of young before commencing to moult in the autumn.

It is very common for Cockatiels to pluck their young, usually on the head but occasionally on other parts of the body, before they leave the nest. This need not give too much cause for worry; unless the plucking has been particularly severe new feathers will grow when the young birds are separated from their parents. Plucking is more likely to occur if the female lays before all the young have left the nest. To try to prevent this happening, two nest-boxes should be hung up at the start of each breeding season and, if the female desires, the second clutch will be laid in the other box.

On leaving the nest some Cockatiels may prove to be very nervous. Three or four days after they are known to be feeding themselves, it is advisable to place nervous birds in a cage, preferably in the house where they will be in the centre of activity. In this way they will quickly become steady and remain so for the rest of their lives. This will be an advantage whether they are intended for pets or for breeding.

There are a number of colour mutations of the Cockatiel which add greatly to their interest. The most beautiful, also the most inexpensive, is the form which has the grey areas of the plumage replaced by white or yellow. Confusingly, it is known variously as White, Albino or Lutino. Whatever name is given to it, this is an extremely beautiful bird, for the contrast between the orange cheeks and the white and yellow body is a striking one. Those contemplating buying a pet Cockatiel should not do so until they have seen a bird of this mutation as many people prefer them to the normal grey Cockatiel. The body colour in this mutation is variable but breeders should be encouraged to select for yellow, that is, to pair together the birds showing the deepest yellow on the breast and to discard for breeding purposes those which are very pale yellow.

Adult birds of this mutation can be sexed by examination of the underside of the tail and flight feathers. These are faintly barred with yellow in the female, pure-white in the male. As with normal Cockatiels, they can be sexed at their first moult, which occurs when they are a few months old.

This mutation is sex-linked in its manner of inheritance. Those familiar with budgerigar genetics will understand what is meant by this term and how to pair the birds to produce young of the same colour.

In birds of sex-linked mutations, a male can carry the factor for the sex-linked colour but visually it is normal in colour. Such birds are described as being 'split' (written /) for the colour they carry. A female bird is either visually normal or sex-linked—she cannot be split for another colour. Thus there are male and female Cockatiels which are White (Albino or Lutino), but only males which are split for White. The result of pairing these birds together is as follows:

White x White = 100% White young

White male x normal grey female

= normal grey/White males) in equal
White females) numbers

Normal grey male x White female

= normal grey/White males) in equal
normal grey females) numbers

Normal grey/White male x White female

= males: White) in equal
normal/White) numbers
females: White) in equal
normal) numbers

It should be understood that the theoretical expectations are as above, but it might not be until a number of nests of young had been reared from one pair that the results would exactly equal the theory. For example, in the first nest from a normal/White male paired to a White female, all the males reared could be normal/White while in the next nest they might all be Whites.

The other mutations of the Cockatiel available have yet to be bred in large numbers; consequently they are more expensive than the White.

A fairly recent mutation is the Pearl which could be equated to the Opaline mutation of the Budgerigar.In the Pearl, which has also been called the Laced, the wing feathers are dark in the centre and white or yellow on the edges to produce a scalloped effect. The appearance of individuals of this mutation is quite variable. The unusual feature of it is that male birds lose the scalloped effect with each moult, until eventually they are normal in appearance except for pale streaks under the wing, near the shoulder. This mutation is sex-linked and the manner of inheritance is therefore the same as described for the White Cockatiel.

The Pied was the first mutation to appear but never attained a great degree of popularity. Its grey plumage is broken by patches of white, especially on the head. This mutation is recessive in its manner of inheritance. This means that both males and females can carry the Pied factor although they are visually normal. When two Pieds are paired together all the young produced will be Pied. When a Pied is paired to a normal all the young will be normal in appearance but will carry the factor for Pied, in other words they are normal/Pied. When two split Pied birds are paired together, the young produced will be Pieds, normals and split Pieds.

The Cinnamon or Isabelle is another sex-linked mutation. Its colour is a pale grey-brown.

Fischers Lovebird

Masked Lovebird

Lovebirds

Next to Cockatiels, lovebirds are the group most likely to be kept by the beginner. They have a number of important attributes—being relatively inexpensive, hardy, easy to care for and very willing to nest in captivity.

The species which are most readily available—Peach-faced, Fischer's and Masked—have one major drawback: they are very difficult to sex by outward appearance. If possible, it is therefore better to obtain four birds at the outset, rather than two pairs of different species. Four birds can be kept together in an aviary—indoors or out—and will soon form pairs if of opposite sexes. Nest-boxes should be provided for roosting and each true pair will roost in a separate box. By blocking the entrance at night the pairs can thus be indentified, and separated if necessary.

Lovebirds are quarrelsome and are normally best kept on their own, but colony breeding has sometimes proved successful—provided that only known true pairs are included in the colony. It is the unmated birds, especially the females, which so often prove to be spiteful.

Lovebirds are very hardy, with the possible exception of the Red-faced, which is seldom available these days. They roost in their nest-boxes which should be left in position throughout the year and this often results in these birds breeding during the winter. The young usually survive, even in the worst weather.

Lovebirds will breed in indoor cages but, under these conditions, there is one problem which is often encountered and which may prove difficult to counteract. The dry atmosphere causes the young to die in the shell which, because of the dryness, is thicker than usual and cannot be penetrated by the chick. Trays of water in the vicinity of the cage will increase the humidity slightly but the problem is more likely to be solved if, during the last few days of the incubation period, the eggs are lightly sprayed or spinkled with warm water. For the same reason, bathing facilities should always be available; some hens will instinctively return to the nest in a saturated condition after bathing.

Unfortunately, however, some lovebird pairs repeatedly fail to produce young even if an attempt is made to provide the correct humidity and, unless they can be placed in an outdoor aviary, they may never breed successfully.

On the subject of keeping lovebirds indoors, it should be noted that these birds are not suitable as pets, for it is extremely rarely that one becomes tame and, like most parrots which are not tame, their life will be far more enjoyable if they are provided with a companion of their own species.

Lovebirds make ideal aviary birds because they are not especially noisy or destructive and, being small, they will thrive and breed in the smallest enclosure. An aviary 1.8m. (6-ft.) long and 75-cm. (2-ft. 6-in.) wide is adequate for one pair and many have reared young in much smaller cages.

The size of nest-box provided should vary according to the species: Peach-faced, Fischer's, Masked, Nyasa and Black-cheeked Lovebirds build a nest using strips of bark from fresh twigs, the remains of millet sprays and dried up greenfood. These birds require a fairly large nest-box and a horizontal oblong type similar to those manufactured for Budgerigars will be suitable. There is no point in providing them with a much larger box as, whatever the size, it will be filled with nesting material, making nest inspection very difficult.

The Abyssinian Lovebird does not build a bulky nest but will gnaw wood from inside the box on which to lay the eggs. The nest-box should be as small as possible, as the provision of one which is too large may prevent these birds from nesting. One successful breeder of these birds uses nest-boxes which measure only 8-cm. (3-in.) square and 23-cm. (9-in.) high.

Lovebirds usually lay four to six eggs in a clutch, although the Madagascar lays larger clutches and the Abyssinian only three eggs. These are incubated by the female for about 23 or 24 days. The chicks are at first covered with down. They leave the nest when between six and seven weeks old, according to the species.

While the chicks are being reared, the parents should be offered bread and milk, to which wheatgerm cereal can be added. The provision of this mixture will make all the difference to the quality of the chicks reared, especially in winter. The usual foods should also be available. These will consist of small seeds, such as canary, millet, a little hemp and niger, also spray millet and sunflower. Apple and greenfoods should be offered daily.

In captivity the most free-breeding species are the Peach-faced, Masked and Fischer's and most of those offered for sale are aviary-bred.

The Peach-faced Lovebird, *Agapornis roseicollis*, is mainly green with most of the face and the upper breast rose-pink and the rump bright blue. The bill is horn coloured. It measures about 16-cm. (6-in.). Male and female are coloured alike. Immature birds have the head greenish tinged with pink and some black markings on the upper mandible.

Several mutations have been firmly established and many more are known. The most popular at the present time is the recessive Blue, which would be more accurately known as the pastel blue; it is mainly sea-green with pale salmon coloured face. Its delicate coloration appeals to many breeders.

The Peach-faced has only a narrow area of white skin surrounding the eye, but this feature is very prominent in the Masked Lovebird, *Agapornis personata* and its sub-species, the Fischer's, Black-cheeked and Nyasa which are often considered as separate species. All have the beak red.

The Masked Lovebird has the head black and the upper breast bright yellow. The upper tail coverts are blue and the tail is marked with orange and black. Size is about 15-cm. (6-in.). The most popular mutation is the blue which is nearly all blue with the head black, the breast whitish and the beak horn coloured. It is recessive in its manner of inheritance.

Fischer's Lovebird, *Agapornis p.fischeri*, has most of the head and upper breast orange, the upper parts dark green and the underparts yellowish-green. The upper tail coverts are dark blue. The latter feature and its slightly larger size distinguishes it from the Nyasa Lovebird, *A.p.lilianae*, which is now rare in captivity. Fischer's Lovebird is about the same size as the Masked which, to avoid confusion with the Black-cheeked Lovebird, should not be called the Black-masked Lovebird.

The Black-cheeked Lovebird, *A.p.nigrigensis*, is now rare in captivity. It has the forehead and crown brown and the cheeks brownish-black. The upper breast is pale orange and the tail is marked with orange and black. It measures about 14-cm. (5½-in.).

In all cases, immature birds are a duller version of the adults with blackish markings on the upper mandible.

The three species which follow are not consistently bred in captivity and most of the birds available will be wild caught. They will therefore need a careful period of acclimatisation if obtained during the colder months. They have the very great advantage of being sexable on sight.

The male Abyssinian Lovebird, *A.taranta*, has the forehead and the beak red, the under wing coverts black and the rest of the plumage green, darker above. The largest of the lovebirds, measuring about 17-cm. (7-in.), it is sometimes known as the Black-winged. However, this feature does not usually apply to the all-green female. Immature birds resemble the female except for the fact that males have black under wing coverts. Young birds have the bill marked with black. The Abyssinian generally proves to be tamer in captivity than the other members of the genus; another advantage is its quieter voice.

The male Madagascar Lovebird, *A.cana*, is instantly recognisable by its pale grey head. It too has black under wing coverts and the tail is barred with black. The bill is pale grey. The all-green female could be mistaken for a parrotlet. Immature birds resemble adults. This is one of the smallest of the lovebirds, measuring about 14-cm. (5½-in.). This species nests readily in captivity, even in a cage, but often tends to nest too late in the year and has not proved to be a successful winter breeder, unlike the Peach-faced for example. Unfortunately, newly imported birds often have air sac mites; a pest which can be killed by placing a dichlorvos strip near the cage.

The Red-faced Lovebird, *A.pullaria*, is the prettiest of the group, to my eyes. It is a particularly pleasing shade of apple green, small and neatly built with a tiny beak and finch-like twitter, being quite incapable of a harsh or loud note. The beak and face are deep orange in the male, paler in the female; the rump is blue and the tail is prettily banded with orange and black. The rest of the plumage is green. The male has the under wing coverts black; the female's are green. This species measures about 14-cm. (5½-in.). It has very rarely been bred in captivity. Although it will use a nest-box, because of its habit of breeding in termites' nests, it seems to need to excavate its own nest to stimulate breeding and a small improvised bale of peat has been provided by successful breeders.

For the sake of completeness, mention is made of the Black-collared or Swinderen's Lovebird, *A.swinderniana*. This species has never been exported as it has proved impossible to keep alive in captivity for more than a few days.

With the exception of the Madagascar, all the lovebirds come from Africa and the supply of the imported species depends very much on the political situation there.

Red-faced Lovebird

Peach-faced Lovebird.

Australian Parakeets

The parakeets from Australia comprise one of the most popular groups of birds with aviculturists. This is mainly because of their beautiful plumage and willingness to breed in captivity. In Europe, including Britain, probably the majority of collections of parrots consist mainly of these birds.

The grass parakeets dislike damp or humid conditions but the other species are very hardy. All Australian parakeets have been captive-bred for generations, as Australia does not allow the export of her native fauna. Many species are completely domesticated and have produced colour mutations, some of which are well established.

These birds are easy to care for and will thrive on a mainly seed diet, except when they are breeding. They will then require extra greenfood and bread and milk. Seeds offered should include sunflower, canary seed, white and panicum millet, hemp and niger. The larger species will also eat peanuts and pine nuts. All will enjoy millet sprays and most will also eat apple, but seldom show much enthusiasm for other fruits. The various wild greenfoods, such as chickweed and seeding grasses, are an important part of the diet.

The Australian parakeets should be considered solely as aviary birds. They are usually most unhappy when confined to a cage. Even hand-reared birds do not make good pets, usually being very aggressive.

Probably the majority of Australian parakeets kept in aviaries carry the parasitic roundworm *Ascaridia hermaphridita*, and this can be a very serious problem in ground feeding birds. For this reason the aviary floor should be of a substance which can be kept free of worm eggs, as explained earlier. The eggs have thick shells and can remain viable for up to 12 months, so it is essential to rid the aviary of the worms as well as treating infected birds. If it is suspected that a bird has worms, its droppings should be examined for worm eggs by a knowledgeable aviculturist or by a laboratory or veterinary surgeon. Unless an affected bird is treated the worms will multiply to such an extent that the intestines will be blocked— a condition which will lead to the bird's death.

Experienced aviculturists dose their birds with a vermifuge such as Nilverm (obtainable from a veterinary surgeon) at least twice annually, usually before and after the breeding season. A veterinary surgeon or experienced aviculturist should demonstrate the method normally used: a syringe with the needle removed and replaced with a length of soft rubber tubing is filled with the appropriate amount of the vermifuge for the bird to be dosed. The rubber tube is placed in the bird's mouth and gently pushed down its throat so that the preparation is directed immediately into the bird's crop. When this method is used there is a risk that birds may die due to shock or incorrect administration. Some aviculturists therefore prefer to put the vermifuge in the birds' drinking water. If this method is used, the birds must be confined to the shelter of the aviary or elsewhere where they cannot quench their thirst in any other manner. A third alternative, if a softfood is eaten such as bread and milk, is to add the vermifuge to it.

The grass parakeets of the genus Neophema are ground feeders and usually need to be treated for worms. They are diminutive birds, measuring about 20-cm. (8-in.) which do well in small aviaries and have quiet voices. They are therefore ideal for those with small gardens and those who live in built-up areas.

The genus includes the delicately coloured Bourke's Parakeet, *N.bourkii*. It has the head and back greyish-brown and the feathers of the wing coverts brown, prominently edged with buff. The underparts are rose pink and pinkish-brown. The under tail coverts and the flanks are sky blue and the male only has the forehead blue. Adult plumage is attained after the first moult which occurs at about four months old. Before this they are a duller version of the female. There are more Bourke's Parakeets in captivity than in their natural habitat, where its numbers have decreased greatly during the past century. However, in captivity it has proved to be one of the most free-breeding of the Australian parakeets. It is usually double-brooded. It is also one of the most charming, with its large dark eyes and semi-crepuscular habits.

Yellow and Isabelle (cinnamon) mutations have been established but they are rare and expensive at the time of writing.

A few years ago the Turquoisine Parakeet, *N.pulchella*, was considered an avicultural rarity; now it is one of the most common and free-breeding of all parakeets. An extremely beautiful bird, it has brilliant almost iridescent turquoise on the face and wings. The underparts and underside of the tail are bright yellow. The rest of

African Ringneck Parakeet

56

Turquoisine Grass Parakeet

the plumage is green, except for the reddish-chestnut patch on the male's wing. The bill is dark brown. The female differs from the male in being duller and has a smaller area of blue on the face. If young birds are examined closely it is often possible to distinguish the males, which may have a few red feathers in the area where the wing bar will later appear, but these birds cannot be sexed with certainty until the first moult, which occurs when they are about five months old.

The Turquoisine and the Splendid or Scarlet-chested Parakeets, *N.splendida*, are both endangered in Australia due to habitat destruction, thus there are far more examples in private collections than there are in the wild.

The Splendid is the gem of the *Neophemas*, the male being one of the most vividly coloured of all parakeets. It can briefly be described as resembling the Turquoisine but lacks the red wing patch and has the upper breast scarlet. The female is easily confused with the female Turquoisine but the blue in her plumage is less vivid. The Splendid is more expensive than the Turquoisine but its price has dropped in recent years, since very large numbers have been bred in Europe.

Less brightly coloured but with a most attractive colour scheme is the Elegant Grass Parakeet, *N.elegans*. This species has more slender proportions than the Splendid and its name is well deserved. It has the back green and the underparts, including the underside of the tail, yellow, except the breast which is yellowish-green. The forehead is dark blue, behind which is a narrow line of turquoise. This colour scheme is repeated on the wings: the margins are dark blue and the wing coverts are turquoise. Some females are as brightly coloured as the male, but most are a duller shade of yellow. However, a distinction can be made by examining the flight feathers which are blue-black in the male and brownish-black in the female. Young birds may or may not show the band of colour on the forehead on leaving the nest, but males usually have the abdomen more yellow. The Elegant is fast gaining in popularity behind the three species described so far.

While the numbers of Elegant Parakeets in captivity have increased in recent years, those of the Blue-winged Grass Parakeet, *N.chrysostoma,* have decreased, perhaps because it is not quite as vividly coloured. It is mainly olive green with pale yellow underparts and dark blue wings. The frontal band is blue and the flight feathers are black in the male. The female has duller blue on the wings and her flight feathers are brownish-black.

Despite their small size and gentle appearance, grass parakeets are extremely aggressive towards others of their own kind or genus, which means that colony breeding is out of the question and that each pair must be given an aviary to itself. It has been proved possible to keep Splendid Parakeets in the same aviary as the large and gentle Princess of Wales' Parakeet; these two species being compatible, they will each carry out their breeding activities entirely successfully. Generally speaking, however, the one pair per aviary rule must be observed.

The *Neophema* parakeets lay four to six eggs, which are incubated by the female for 19 days. Young birds leave the nest when they are between four and five weeks old. It sometimes happens that they leave the nest too early, before they are able to fly. It is then advisable to shut them in the shelter with the parents.

Most young *Neophemas* are extremely nervous on fledging, so much so that precautions must be taken to prevent them flying into the wire netting and seriously or fatally injuring themselves. Some breeders place plenty of twiggy branches at the end of the flight, and one that I know ties pieces of cloth to the wire. A more natural idea is to allow a climbing plant, such as honeysuckle or clematis, to grow over the end of the aviary. One advantage of housing these birds in small aviaries, with the flight only about 1.8m. (6-ft.) or 2.4m. (8-ft.) long, is that young birds cannot gain sufficient impetus to hit the wire at speed.

Another danger on fledging is the animosity shown by some males, especially Turquoisines, towards their male offspring. It may be necessary to remove them immediately they are feeding themselves, to prevent the male parent injuring them.

Nest-boxes for these birds should measure approximately 15-cm. (6-in.) square and at least 26-cm. (10-in.) deep. The depth is important as young are less likely to leave the nest prematurely in a fairly deep box.

Many grass parakeets become very tame and steady and are therefore more interesting to keep than some of the larger parakeets. Most are double-brooded, many are prolific, and the sale of their young will not only cover the cost of feeding them, but of keeping other birds in the collection.

The genus *Psephotus* consists of one species which is extremely well-known in captivity, the Red-rumped Parakeet; one which is moderately well-known, the Many-coloured; two which are extremely rare and beautiful, the Hooded and the Golden-shouldered; and the Paradise Parakeet which, unfortunately, is almost certainly extinct.

The Red-rumped Parakeet, *P.haematonotus*, is inexpensive and free-breeding, thus invariably recommended for the beginner. On no account should it be housed with other birds, for this species is extremely aggressive during the breeding season.

Adult and young birds can be sexed at a glance – a very great advantage. The male is far more colourful, being mainly green above, brownish-green on the mantle and red on the rump. There is a yellow patch on the wing, just below the shoulder, and the under wing coverts and the outer edges of the primaries are blue. The tail is brownish-green above and greyish-white below. Yellow is the colour of the underparts. The length of this species is about 27-cm. (10½-in.).

In comparison, the female is drably coloured, being mainly brownish-green with some blue feathers on the edge of the wing.

Young birds can be sexed even before they leave the nest as males have some red feathers on the rump and green on the head. Occasionally a young female will show red on the rump, but will not be green on the head.

The Yellow Red-rump is well established. It is badly named for it is a dilute mutation. The male is not bright yellow but a dilute edition of the green in which only the rump retains its brilliant colour. The female is creamy-yellow. This mutation is sex-linked. This species generally proves to be a very reliable breeder and can be used to foster the young of other parakeets if the necessity arises.

The Rosella Parakeets *(Platycercus)* form one of the most brilliantly coloured groups of birds in the world and they have long been great favourites with aviculturists. They need more flying space than the smaller parakeets: flights should be 4.8m. (16-ft.) in length and preferably 6m. (20-ft.) for the Pennant's Parakeet.

Some species or individuals are difficult to sex by the plumage coloration, in which case the shape of the head provides a guide; the male has more frontal rise (over the eye) and, when viewed from the front, the beak is seen to be larger and broader.

These birds will breed when only one year old but two year old birds are generally more satisfactory. They should be provided with nest-boxes which are approximately 25-cm. (10-in.) to 31-cm. (12-in.) square and 60-cm. (2-ft.) to 1.2m. (4-ft.) deep. As with the *Neophemas*, the deeper the box, the less chance there is of the young leaving the nest prematurely. The entrance hole should be about 7-cm. (3-in.) in diameter and should be placed about 15-cm. (6-in.) from the top of the box. Half inch plywood is a suitable material from which to construct it.

Rosellas lay four to eight eggs, which are incubated by the female for about 19 days. When the chicks are about 10 days old they start to feather up and to separate from the cluster which they have previously formed. At about six weeks old they leave the nest and should be left with their parents for at least six weeks—if the male will tolerate their presence. One specialist breeder of these birds found that the longer the young were left with their parents, the more satisfactory they proved as breeders.

Some male Rosellas, and Australian parakeets of other species, prove so aggressive towards the female when they come into breeding condition, that it is necessary to cut the primaries on one of the male's wings to prevent him chasing the hen.

The most common Rosella in captivity is the Red or Eastern, *P.eximius*. Aviculturists almost invariably refer to it as the Golden-mantled Rosella, a name which should be reserved for the sub-species *cecilae* in which the feathers of the back and mantle are edged with gold. So much interbreeding between the two races has occurred in captivity that few pure birds exist.

This very colourful parakeet has the head scarlet, except for a white patch extending from the cheeks to the throat; the upper breast and the area surrounding the vent are also scarlet. Yellow is the colour of the abdomen. The feathers of the back are black with yellow edges, the wings are mainly blue and the rump is light green or bluish-green, the upper tail coverts being similarly coloured. The tail is dark blue above and light blue on the underside. The Red Rosella measures about 30-cm. (12-in.).

Coloration of females is variable; some are almost as brightly coloured as the male, thus this species is often difficult to sex. Usually, but not always, the red on the head and breast is duller and the white on the cheeks is less pure in shade, nearer pale grey than white. These birds can usually be sexed with accuracy by taking them in the hand and examining the underside of the wing. Young birds and females have a row of white spots which the males lose at a year old (when they moult into adult plumage) or, in some cases, when they are two years old. Immature birds have the head and neck mainly green with a few red feathers—usually more in the males.

Like Red-rumps, Red Rosellas make good foster parents for other large parakeets. They often prove prolific and rear nests of seven or eight young; nine is not unknown.

The smallest of the Rosellas is also one of the most attractive—the Stanley Parakeet or Western Rosella *P.icterotis*. They have several advantages as aviary birds, including the quieter melodious voice and their friendly disposition. Also, they will thrive in aviaries only 3m. (10-ft.) long. They generally prove to be free breeders but, unlike most Rosellas, are usually single-brooded.

The Stanley Parakeet has yellow cheek patches but is otherwise red on the head and underparts. The underside of the tail is pale blue and the upper surface is greenish-blue. The back is green, the feathers of the mantle being black with green edges. The wings are green and blue. Length of this species is only 25-cm. (10-in.).

While most female Stanley Parakeets are much duller than the males, especially on the underparts where the red feathers may be mingled with a few green ones, and the yellow cheek patch is usually less extensive, there are females which are almost as brightly coloured as the male.

Immature birds are mainly green, with some reddish-brown feathers on the forehead which, in young males, are usually darker in colour. Males do not attain full adult plumage until the second moult.

The Pennant's Parakeet, *P.elegans*, is an extremely handsome bird, recognised by its large size—36-cm. (14-in.)—and mainly crimson and blue plumage. It has the head, except for the blue patch on the cheeks and throat, crimson, also the entire underparts. The feathers of the back are black, edged with red and the tail is mainly blue, also the edges of the wings.

This species is difficult to sex as females are usually as brilliantly coloured as the males and not all show the row of white spots on the underside of the wing. Size is not a reliable guide to their sex either. Probably the best indicator is the size of the head and the beak, which is normally larger in male birds.

Immature plumage is extremely variable. Some birds are mainly green with some red on the head, while others more nearly resemble adults, being mostly red but of a duller shade.

It is a hardy and beautiful bird and is often known as the Crimson Rosella. However, they are, on the whole, not such reliable breeders in captivity. Some hens will lay but not incubate and it is therefore worthwhile fostering the eggs to Red Rosellas kept specially for this purpose. This species usually proves to be more destructive to woodwork than the smaller Rosellas. Because of its less certain breeding abilities and its higher price, it is not recommended for the beginner.

The Rosellas described so far are predominantly red in coloration, but some members of the genus have little or no scarlet in the plumage. One such bird is the Mealy Rosella, *P.adscitus*, which is sometimes known as the Pale-headed Rosella. Its colour scheme is predominantly yellow, blue and white. The head is pale yellow with white cheek patches and the upper breast is yellow. The abdomen is light blue, also the underside of the tail, and the under tail coverts are scarlet. The feathers of the mantle are black, edged with golden-yellow. There is a black patch on the shoulder and the edge of the wing is blue. The tail is dark blue above. This species measures about 30-cm. (12-in.).

Coloration is variable but those with the richest colours are very attractive birds. However, sexing frequently causes problems. Some females are duller, especially on the under tail coverts, but this does not always apply. One experienced breeder of this species found that the male usually has a broader, flatter head, larger eyes and a thicker neck.

These active birds need a flight at least 4.5m. (15-ft.) in length. Failure to provide an adequate aviary may be the reason why some aviculturists have not found it easy to breed, because when well-housed, it often proves to be a prolific breeder and, more often than not, is double-brooded.

The other Rosellas are less often found in captivity, thus they are more expensive. These are: Tasmanian or Yellow-bellied Rosella, *P. caledonicus caledonicus;*Yellow or Yellow-rumped Rosella, *P.c.flaveolus* and the Northern Rosella or Brown's Parakeet, *P.venustus.*

There are four other genera of exclusively Australian parakeets, the members of which are expensive and seldom as free-breeding as those already described.

The Red-capped or Pileated Parakeet, *Purpureicephalus spurius,* is the only member of its genus. A beautiful bird, but rather shy, it needs a lengthy aviary. It has always been rather rare in captivity. It is mainly green with mauve breast, lime green cheeks and a red cap.

The Blue-bonnet Parakeets are sometimes placed in a separate genus, *Northiella,* while some taxonomists place them with the genus *Psephotus.* The Blue-bonnet Parakeet, *P.haematogaster,* has several races, known to aviculturists as the Yellow-vented, Red-vented and Little or Naretha Blue-bonnet.

These birds are noted for their aggressiveness and should never be kept with even large birds. A pair I once saw which were housed with Pheasants constantly chased and persecuted their larger companions.

Blue-bonnets are dull olive-green, with the face, shoulder, wings and tail tip blue and the abdomen red and yellow. They measure about 28-cm. (11-in.). The male has more red on the abdomen than the female; in the hen the red feathers are edged with yellow. Immature birds are dull versions of the adults.

Two species which are mainly attired in shades of green, bluish-green and yellow are the Barnard's and Port Lincoln Parakeets. Formerly included in the genus *Platycercus,* they are now placed in a separate genus, *Barnardius.* Barnard's Parakeet, *B.barnardi,* has the forehead red, cheeks light blue, yellow collar and yellow abdomen. The wings are green, with blue on the primaries and the back is blackish-blue. The rest of the plumage is green. This species measures 33-cm. (13-in.). The sub-species, *macgillivrayi,* known as the Cloncurry Parakeet, which lacks the red forehead, has bright blue ear coverts and a wide band of yellow on the abdomen. It is rare in aviculture and extremely expensive. In both birds the female is duller than the male and has the back dark greyish-green.

The Port Lincoln Parakeet, *B.zonarius,* is a very handsome bird of bold appearance. It measures about 38-cm. (15-in.). It has the head black, a yellow collar on the nape, bluish-green upper breast and brilliant green rump and wings. The abdomen is yellow and the tail is dark green. These birds are difficult to sex; sometimes the head is more brownish in the female.

The sub-species *semitorquatus* is known as the Twenty-eight Parakeet. It has a prominent crimson frontal band and the abdomen is green.

Their graceful outline, beauty and tameness commend the *Polytelis* parakeets to the experienced aviculturist. The Barraband's Parakeet, *P. swainsonii,* is not as brightly coloured the Rosellas, for example, but many would consider the male to be more beautiful. The ill-fitting name Green Leek Parrot is sometimes bestowed on it in Australia.

The male is mainly green with the forehead and cheeks yellow and a crescent of red on the throat, extending to below the ear coverts. The underside of the tail is black and the beak is coral-red. This species measures 40-cm. (16-in.). There are no sexing problems here as the female is mainly green, of a duller shade, with red feathers on the thighs and pink inner webs to the tail feathers. She is of less slender proportions. Immature birds are mainly green with some brown feathers on the throat, usually more in males.

The Princess of Wales' Parakeet, *P. alexandrae,* is a most beautiful bird, of similar proportions to and slightly larger than the Barraband's; it measures about 45-cm. (18-in.). Much of this length is accounted for by the very long tail. The delicate pastel tones of its plumage and its delightful disposition have long made it a favourite with aviculturists. It is so gentle that it can be housed with small birds. This parakeet does not have a reputation for being free-breeding in captivity. Although it often nests readily, many problems are encountered. Another drawback is the voice, which is rather irritating and persistent.

The male is mainly dull olive-green with the top of the head, also the rump, blue. The throat and the sides of the head and neck are pink and the edge of the wing is bright green. The abdomen is bluish-grey and the inner webs of the tail feathers are pink. The beak is red. The female is much duller; she has the crown greyish-blue and a much shorter tail. A blue mutation exists but specimens are rare.

The Rock Peppler or Rock Peplar Parakeet, *P. anthopeplus,* known as the 'Smoker' in Australia, is mainly yellow with the mantle dark green, the inner wing coverts red and the flight feathers blue and black. The tail is black on the upper surface and pink on the inner webs. The female is mainly olive green, as are immature birds.

The *Polytelis* parakeets do best in flights which are 6m. (20-ft.) in length. They often need deep natural logs to induce them to nest. Unfortunately they are rather prone to paralysis of the legs.

Due to their high price and the greater difficulties in breeding from them, the King Parakeets *(Alisterus)* and the Crimson-winged Parakeets *(Aprosmictus)* from Australia and New Guinea should be considered suitable only for the experienced aviculturist.

Barraband Parakeet (left)
Princess-of-Wales Parakeet (right)

Ring-necked Parakeets

Easily the best-known member of the large family of *Psittacula* parakeets from Asia is the Ring-necked Parakeet. It is a bird of elegant proportions with a very long tail. In flight it looks superb as many people outside its native India are well aware; there are feral populations of this species in a number of countries, including England.

Ring-necked Parakeets are also found in Africa — thus this is the only parrot to be found in two continents. The male Indian Ring-neck, *P. krameri manillensis,* is immediately distinguished from the female by the narrow line of black feathers which encircles the neck and throat. Two pastel coloured lines, one salmon-pink, the other pale blue, follow the black ring. There is another narrow line of black on the forehead. The beak is dark red. The rest of the plumage is green. Females and immature birds are entirely green.

The African Ring-necked Parakeet, *P. k. krameri,* differs in its slightly smaller size and in having a much darker red beak. The tail is not quite as long as in the Indian Ring-neck but the proportions are perhaps even more graceful. In the Indian species the long tail accounts for about half the total length of 43-cm. (17-in.).

Males obtain adult plumage when between two and three years old, when many an assumed female will reveal its true identity. For some unknown reason, in Ring-neck Parakeets and in other members of the genus, males far outnumber females. The explanation of this fact may have been discovered by G.A. Smith, who regularly weighed the chicks hatched by his pairs. He found that the males grow more quickly than the females and can be as much as half as heavy again for the first three weeks of their lives. It therefore follows that male chicks have a better chance of survival.

The great preponderance of imported males may have been one reason why, in the past, so many were released to form feral flocks. Also it has often happened that those who know little about parrots have been persuaded to buy an adult male Ring-neck in the guise of a 'baby talking parrot'. Unfortunately, adult Ring-necks are almost impossible to tame and certainly will not learn to talk. In any case, they are most unsuited to cage life, being far too active to lead that kind of existence.

Ring-necks are among the easiest parakeets to breed in aviaries, once one has a located a female. More than one pair can be kept in a large aviary as the males defend only the area in the immediate vicinity of their nest – but the females are less tolerant.

In Ring-neck pairs, the female is very much the dominant bird, except for the brief period of courtship. It usually takes a male some time to lose his fear of the female, which is why two birds must be put together several months in advance of the breeding season, which starts in February. The pair bond is not maintained out of the breeding season; there will then be no mutual preening or affectionate behaviour.

The male's courtship display, which is performed to recreate the pair bond before the breeding season, is accompanied by melodious notes which are more pleasant than the usual harsh call notes. After preening the hen, he blazes his eyes, pulls his head back and raises it high, shoots his head forward, lifts his foot high off the perch, then flies off. On the ground he walks with an exaggerated gait and hops around the hen with eyes blazing, in a manner which is most amusing to observe.

Because Ring-necks are such early nesters, the nest-box must be in position by the end of January. If prevented from breeding then, the hen may not lay at all. Three or four eggs are laid on a nest lining of a few splinters of gnawed wood and perhaps some feathers. Incubation is carried out by the female and lasts for 26 days. The chicks are almost naked on hatching; their eyes open when they are about 10 days old. The young birds leave the nest when they are about eight weeks old and are independent three weeks later. If the hen's eggs are removed or lost for some reason, she will usually lay a second clutch but will not do so if chicks are reared.

Two mutations of the Indian Ring-neck Parakeet are well established in captivity. Both are extremely beautiful. The lutino (a sex-linked mutation) is pure yellow; the male retains the pink and black neck ring.

The blue mutation of the Ring-neck is, perhaps, the loveliest mutation in any parrot. The shade is a most pleasing powder blue. Its manner of inheritance is recessive.

A few albino Ring-necks have been bred. Several other mutations, such as the cinnamon, have been established, but are far less striking than the lutino and the blue and are never likely to attain the same degree of popularity. The blue is the most expensive of all and well beyond the pocket of the average aviculturist.

Ring-necks are easy birds to cater for. They will consume all the usual seeds – sunflower, peanuts, canary, millet and hemp. Every day some greenfood and or fruit should be provided. Being long-lived birds, many individuals reach their twenties. They are very hardy except in one respect – they are very susceptible to frost bite, which will cause the loss of their toes. They should therefore be persuaded to roost in the shelter every night.

The foregoing remarks apply equally to the other members of the genus. One of my favourites is the Alexandrine Parakeet, *P.eupatria*. It can briefly be described as a very large version of the Ring-neck, differing only in the red shoulder patch. Half of the total length of 58-cm. (23-in.) is accounted for by the long tail.

Alexandrines are very intelligent birds, equalling the larger parrots in this respect. The principal drawback as aviary birds is their extreme destructiveness; they are quite as demolition-minded as cockatoos. Despite this fault, they are worth a place in any collection. Even more long-lived than Ring-necks, a breeding pair will rear young consistently, or almost so, for over 20 years. The usual clutch is two eggs. If obtained when young an Alexandrine will make a tame and interesting pet and will learn to repeat a few words.

Perhaps the best-known member of the genus, next to the Ring-necked Parakeet, is the Plum-headed Parakeet, *P.cyanocephala*. The problem of obtaining females seems to be even more acute in this species than in the Ring-neck. The male has the head plum-coloured; the narrow black neck ring and small red wing patch are present. The female is mainly green with the head bluish-grey. Length of this species is 36-cm. (14-in.). This is the smallest of the genus and one of the most beautiful.

Frequently available is the Moustache Parakeet, *P.alexandri fasciata*. The male has the head blue-grey with a prominent black moustache. The breast is deep pink and the central tail feathers are blue with the tip yellow. The beak is red in the male and black in the female. The rest of the plumage is green. This species measures about 40-cm. (15-in.).

The Long-tailed Parakeet, *P.longicauda,* is occasionally imported from Malaya. In this species, both sexes are most attractively marked. The male has the cheeks and the back of the head deep salmon pink – a lovely contrast to the dark green crown and broad black moustache. The rump and lower back are pale blue. The upper mandible is red and the lower mandible black in the male. The female has the beak entirely black. Her crown and lower cheeks are dark green and the upper cheeks are dull orange. Her tail is shorter than the males. Total length is about 40-cm. (16-in.).

Nanday Conure

Cockatoos

Cockatoos are instantly recognised by their predominantly white or black plumage and by their crests—with the exception of two birds which are virtually unknown in aviculture, the Horned Parakeet from New Caledonia and the Uvaen Parakeet from the Loyalty Islands, no other parrots are crested. The Cockatiel, which with its long tail resembles a parakeet, is also a member of the cockatoo family.

The white cockatoos are the best-known species and there can be few people who are not familiar with the Greater Sulphur-crested Cockatoo from Australia, famed for its intelligence and longevity. There are a number of authentic records of cockatoos which have reached ages which would be considered more than remarkable in a human being. The most famous of these veterans was 'Cocky Bennett', reputed to be 119 years old at the time of its death in Australia. It was then a grotesque sight, featherless and with overgrown beak reaching to its breast. While some of these longevity claims may be exaggerated or hard to prove, there is no doubt that some cockatoos have reached exceptional ages.

All the white cockatoos have the underside of the wings or tail tinged with yellow and some have the bases of the feathers of the crest and lores tinged with pink. One bird, however, is remarkable for the exquisite combination of pink, yellow and white in its plumage and is generally considered to be the most beautiful of all cockatoos. It is also one of the most expensive and commands an extremely high price. This is the Leadbeater's or Major Mitchell's Cockatoo from Australia. Sadly, its numbers there have been affected by habitat destruction.

Most cockatoos are expensive to purchase and tame birds naturally fetch a high price. Two of the less expensive species which are suitable as aviary birds are the Lesser Sulphur-crested, *Cacatua sulphurea sulphurea* and the Goffin's Cockatoo, *Cacatua sanguinea goffini*. The former also makes a good pet if obtained when young. Goffin's Cockatoo seldom settles down to cage life. It measures about 30-cm. (12-in.) and, with the Red-vented Cockatoo from the Philippines, is the smallest of the cockatoos, and the Lesser Sulphur-crested is only slightly larger. While they are less noisy than the larger cockatoos, they are still noisy birds by any standards.

The Lesser has a curved crest of lemon yellow, while the Goffin's crest, which is white (except at the base, where it is salmon-pink) and helmet-shaped, normally lies close to the head and is not apparent. When the bird lands on a perch it invariably erects the small crest, also in display when the wings are opened, the crest erected and a shrieking call made in unison.

The Goffin's is a charming little cockatoo found only in the Tenimber Islands. Of recent years it has been imported in large numbers because of deforestation there; it could well become endangered in the not too distant future and aviculturists should therefore make every attempt to breed from the Goffin's Cockatoos in their possession.

Lesser Sulphur-crested have long been one of the most commonly exported of all cockatoos, yet breeding successes with this species (or any other cockatoo for that matter) have not been frequent.

The Greater Sulphur-crested Cockatoo is not available from its country of origin, because for many years Australia has prohibited the export of its native fauna (with the exception of zoo-bred species which may be imported by overseas zoos). Most of the Greater Sulphur-crests seen are therefore quite old birds, as this species is not often bred in captivity.

There are several sub-species which greatly resemble it which are exported from Indonesia and are often given the name of 'Medium' Sulphur-crested Cockatoos by dealers. One such bird is the Triton Cockatoo, *Cacatua galerita triton,* which can be distinguished from the Greater by the area of blue skin surrounding the eye (but should not be confused with the rarely imported Blue-eyed Cockatoo, *C.g.ophthalmica,* from New Britain, which has deeper blue skin surrounding the eye and a different type of crest).

One of the most beautiful of the white cockatoos is the Moluccan, *Cacatua moluccensis.* It is an imposing bird, about 50-cm. (20-in.) long, with a magnificent crest of broad salmon-pink feathers. The white underparts are tinged with pink and the underside of the flight feathers is washed with deep salmon at the base. The tail feathers are pale orange on the undersides. As in the other cockatoos so far described the eye is black in males and brown or reddish-brown in adult females.

The Moluccan Cockatoo must have inspired the desire to own a parrot in many individuals. Tame birds often prove to be quite extraordinarily affectionate and docile. But a word of warning is necessary here. The large cockatoos have ear-splitting voices which few people can tolerate in a house; if they do not receive adequate attention they will not hesitate to use them—in a manner which is likely to draw complaints from neighbours.

Unless they are extremely tame and much time can be devoted to them, cockatoos are best housed in an aviary. It is worth labouring the point that aviaries for these birds must be extremely strong. Small cockatoos are quite as destructive as the large ones; in fact, the little Goffin's is the most destructive parrot I have ever kept. Neither does it confine its attentions to the aviary framework, but will pull staples out of wire and nails from the metal strips used to protect the woodwork.

Cockatoos must be provided with logs or branches to gnaw, especially in an aviary of metal construction. These are absolutely essential for their well-being.

These birds will keep in good condition on a diet consisting of various seeds and greenfoods; some birds will eat fruit but others show no interest in it. Many are very fond of foods in the ear such as wheat, millet sprays and corn-on-the-cob. Cockatoos are often very reluctant to sample new foods and for that reason can often be a problem when they hatch young because they fail to take the necessary nutritious foods.

White cockatoos and Cockatiels are the only parrots (with the exception of certain small lories) in which incubation is shared, the cocks incubating during the day and the hens during the night. The incubation period varies between about 25 and 32 days, according to the species, the shortest period being recorded in the Roseate Cockatoo and the longest in the Moluccan. The young spend a corresponding period in the nest, about 50 days in the Roseate and about 12 weeks in the Moluccan.

The best nesting site for these destructive birds is an oak barrel. An ordinary nest-box can be provided but the interior will have to be reinforced with welded mesh. Stout logs are very acceptable from the birds' point of view, but inspection may prove difficult.

Although a mated pair of cockatoos are extremely affectionate in their behaviour towards each other and will spend hours in mutual preening, finding two birds which are compatible can sometimes be a problem. When two cockatoos are introduced for the first time they must be carefully observed for a while to ensure that should one attack the other, they can be parted at once.

The magnificent black cockatoos from Australia, such as the Banksian and the Funereal, are among the most imposing and interesting of all parrots, but they are rare in aviculture and not likely to be available to private aviculturists.

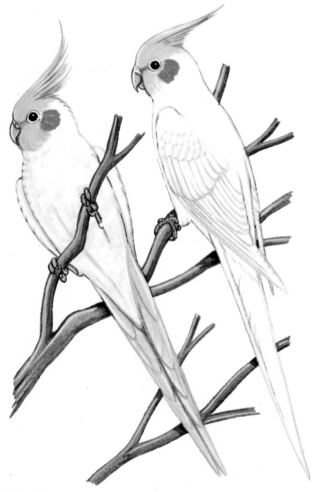

White Cockatiels

Macaws

Imposing, magnificent and spectacular – the large macaws are seldom referred to without one or other of these adjectives. But not all macaws are large, any more than all cockatoos are white. They range in size from the 100-cm. (40-in.) Hyacinthine Macaw, the largest (by length) of all parrots, to the Noble or Red-shouldered Macaw which measures only 30-cm. (12-in.). Of the 16 species in existence, eight exceed 70-cm. (23-in.) in length.

The Hyacinthine, with its glossy rich cobalt plumage, has been described as the most beautiful of all parrots; certainly it is spectacular, but its disproportionately large beak and ungainly manner of moving when not in the air, convinces me that this title should go to a parrot with a more graceful beauty. My own choice would be the Papuan Lorikeet, *Charmosyna papou,* with its long slender tail feathers fluttering behind it like yellow streamers.

Of the large macaws, two are extremely well-known: the Blue and Yellow, *Ara ararauna,* and the scarlet, *Ara macao.* The latter sometimes known as the Red and Yellow Macaw. Both are extremely beautiful birds and I have often felt that were they as rare in captivity as the blue macaws they would be even more highly prized than they already are.

They are offered for sale more often than the other large macaws, but their price is very high. Their beauty and spectacular appearance often attracts the attention of those who have never previously kept birds, leading to a strong desire to keep one, but all too often it proves to be a grave mistake for those without previous experience of bird-keeping to purchase such a bird. Experience should always be gained with the less expensive species – and with those which are less demanding.

Tame macaws, like tame cockatoos, should be left on their own as little as possible. If neglected, they scream or pluck their feathers, and perhaps start this habit by removing the magnificent tail feathers. It is extremely difficult to stop this except by altering the bird's circumstances so that it no longer suffers from boredom. A bird which is not too seriously plucked can be placed in an outdoor aviary, preferably with a mate of its own kind. It is seldom that the distraction provided by the company of another macaw and life in an outdoor aviary does not cure its habit of plucking.

But prevention is better than cure—and it is very wrong to purchase one of these birds as an ornament or status symbol. Few people these days have the necessary time to devote to one of these birds and most captive macaws will fare much better in an outdoor aviary where they have the opportunity to breed.

All those who are familiar with the large macaws cannot fail to be impressed by their dignity and intelligence and what can only be described as 'presence'. They possess these attributes to a higher degree than almost any other bird, thus it is not surprising that they quickly become bored if caged and given insufficient attention.

They make excellent aviary birds and some pairs breed readily. The main difficulty lies in procuring a true pair, for the plumage is alike in both male and female. The behaviour of these birds is not always an obvious indication of their sex. Two of the same sex could be as compatible as a true pair, and when a male and a female are introduced, serious fighting may occur and it may be many months before the two birds live together on friendly terms.

Despite their large size, an aviary for a pair of macaws does not have to be large; in fact, most breeding successes occur in fairly small aviaries. An aviary 3m. (10-ft.) long and 1.5m. (5-ft.) wide would be adequate for a pair, and even one of that size is by no means essential.

Macaws can be very destructive and the same precautions regarding reinforcing the aviary and nest-box should be made as described for cockatoos.

Macaws, like all the large parrots, become extremely aggressive when breeding and may attack anyone who enters their aviary. The large species lay two or three eggs which are incubated by the female for 26 to 28 days. Chicks are almost naked on hatching and look most ungainly with their large head and beak.

Development of the chicks is slow as they remain in the nest for 10 or 11 weeks. During this period it is essential to provide a variety of nutritious foods from which the adult birds can make their choice. Items can include bread and milk, corn-on-the-cob and other fresh vegetables and soaked dog biscuits or monkey chow. At all times macaws should be offered sunflower seed and pine nuts, plus a variety of other nuts, including peanuts, walnuts and Brazils. The ease with which they can open them is fascinating to watch. Most macaws are very fond of fruit and should be offered a wide variety, together with the usual greenfoods. Chop bones and cooked meat will also be relished.

The smaller macaws require a similar diet, except for the large nuts. Less brightly coloured than the large species, they are often known as 'dwarf' macaws. Young birds make superb pets, being playful and affectionate, and are far more suitable for the average household than the large species.

They include the Yellow-naped Macaw, *Ara auricollis,* which is mainly green with a yellow band across the nape; the Severe Macaw, *Ara severa,* also mainly green and with a chestnut forehead; and the prettily marked Illiger's Macaw, *Ara maracana,* which has the forehead and a patch on the abdomen scarlet and the crown and cheeks blue. These three species measure in the region of 40-cm. (16-in.) and there are smaller macaws which are smaller than some conures. They can be distinguished from the latter by the area of bare skin on the cheeks.

All macaws, large and small species, are noisy birds with harsh and penetrating voices and this point needs to be kept in mind by those in built-up areas.

Some of the small macaws have proved to be prolific breeders in captivity. The clutch usually consists of three eggs which are incubated for about 26 days. The period the young spend in the nest varies, being about eight weeks in the small Hahn's Macaw, and up to three months in the larger macaws.

Blue-and-yellow Macaw

Hyacinthe Macaw

Red and yellow Macaw

Lories and Lorikeets

Included among the lories and lorikeets are some of the most beautiful birds in the world; they are nearly all brightly coloured and some are quite spectacular. However, it is not only their appearance which is so attractive but their personalities. They are extremely active and playful and many become very tame. They also nest readily in captivity.

The names lories and lorikeets are interchangeable but, on the whole, the long-tailed or smaller birds are called lorikeets and those with short, square tails are called lories. The birds in this group are small to medium-sized parrots found in New Guinea, Australia and Indonesia.

All have one factor in common: their tongues are specially adapted to feed on pollen, thus they are sometimes known as the 'brush-tongued' parrots, because brush-like papillae on the tongue are erected when they feed. When a lory is not feedings its tongue appears no different from that of any other parrot. It is not until the tongue is extended to reach into a flower or blossom to extract the pollen and nectar that its unique characteristics become apparent.

The range and combination of colours found in lories is not surpassed in the whole avian kingdom. In most lories, red and green are the dominant plumage colours, often complemented with bright patches of other colours. One of my favourites is the Duivenbode's Lory, *Chalcopsitta duivenbodei*. This species from New Guinea, which is not often imported, has, in my opinion, the most beautiful combination of colours of any member of the parrot family. I often gaze at my own pair, spellbound by the rich brown and gold plumage, set off by touches of violet. The face is encircled by a line of gold and when the wings are opened in flight or display (in which I have seen the male revolve around the perch, hanging below it with wings outstretched), the rich gold of the undersides is revealed.

In most lories the plumage is alike in male and female and this, unfortunately, applies to all the species which are likely to be available to the aviculturist. Obtaining a true pair is therefore the major obstacle to be overcome in breeding from them, as it is rarely that true pairs do not attempt to breed. Most lories lay two, occasionally three, eggs and the incubation period is 23 to 26 days, according to the species. The young spend between nine and 12 weeks in the nest.

They are among the most interesting and entertaining of all parrots to keep in an aviary and young birds are a joy to watch for their playfulness. Even adults indulge in all kinds of acrobatics and mock fights, rolling over locked together or swinging by one foot from a branch. Lories move about in a series of jerky movements in complete contrast to the slow, deliberate manner of most of the larger parrots.

Their diet in captivity consists mainly of a simulated nectar and this results in copious droppings, which makes them quite unsuitable for life in a cage. In any case, they are too active to be caged permanently.

In captivity, some lories feed entirely on nectar or nectar and fruit, while others also take seed. However, I believe that seed is essential only for certain small species such as the Iris Lorikeet, *Glossopsitta iris,* which are not generally obtainable. Unless fed in small quantities, seed may possibly do more harm than good to the larger lories.

Almost no two lory keepers use the same 'recipe' for nectar, which can contain almost any nutritious food. Ingredients and method of preparation of the nectar which I use for my lories is as follows:

two heaped dessert-spoonfuls of glucose are dissolved in hot or boiling water, to which is added a dessert-spoonful of malt extract; this is stirred thoroughly and cold water is added to make one litre (35 fluid oz.). To this is added half or a quarter dessert-spoonful of condensed milk (this should be omitted in hot weather or in a warm climate) and a dessert-spoonful of a baby cereal or wheat-germ cereal.

The birds also receive apple, grapes, soft pear and greenfood.

A contrasting and very successful diet is used at San Diego Zoo, which has unparalleled breeding successes with lories. There, various items are made into a soupy mixture. These include cane sugar, a human protein-vitamin-mineral concentrate, chopped apples, boiled rice, soaked raisins, ground carrots, white bread, evaporated milk and shredded lettuce, mixed with water.

There is less wastage of fruit if this is placed in a blender and then added to the nectar. With the use of a blender many kinds of nutritious foods can be included.

While my lories are rearing young, they are offered milk in a separate container, to ensure there is adequate calcium in the diet. This is readily taken.

Lories usually prove to be hardy birds, once acclimatised. The nest-box is always used for roosting, thus this should be left in position throughout the year. This often results in lories nesting at an unseasonable time of year and the young usually succumb if hatched during cold weather. If circumstances allow they can be removed from the nest at the age of one week for hand-rearing. All too often lories pluck their young in the nest—another reason why hand-rearing is sometimes to be preferred.

Most of the lories available to aviculturists are imported birds. Very few have been captive-bred for generations. One exception is the Swainson's Lorikeet, *Trichoglossus haematod moluccanus,* from Australia. This beautiful bird measures about 31-cm. (12-in.) long. It has the head rich blue, almost violet, with blue shaft-streaking on the feathers; the abdomen is the same colour. The nuchal collar is yellowish-green and the breast and flanks are irregularly marked with red and yellow. The upper parts and the thighs are rich green, also the tail. The under tail coverts and the underside of the tail are yellow and green. The under wing coverts are orange. Eyes and beak are deep coral red. In immature birds, the eyes and the beak are brown.

Other Parrots

There are about 330 species of parrots in existence; only an approximate figure can be given as taxonomists do not always agree on the dividing line between species and sub-species. Of these 330, about 240 are known in aviculture. Obviously, in a book of this size it is not possible to cover them all, thus suggestions for further reading are given in the appendix.

The birds discussed in this chapter are all well-known in captivity, but have little else in common other than the fact that they are not included among the species already covered.

Undoubtedly the best-known of the true parrots are the African Grey and certain species of Amazons. Until fairly recent years they were neglected by aviculturists, most birds imported being destined as house pets.

The attributes of the African Grey Parrot, *Psittacus erithacus,* as a pet have been discussed. It also has much to recommend it as an aviary bird, not being as noisy as Amazons for example.

My own pair are housed in an aviary 4.2m. (14-ft.) long and 1.2m. (4-ft.) wide but spend more time climbing than flying about, so a smaller aviary would be quite adequate.

The main difficulty in breeding from Greys is in sexing them, as plumage is alike in male and female. Both birds have the body plumage grey (the actual shade being variable) and the tail red. Some males have an obviously masculine appearance, with large head, feet and beak, but this is by no means always so.

Although breeding successes with this species are becoming more frequent, they cannot be described as very common. A small barrel makes an ideal nesting site. Three or four eggs are laid, occasionally five; the incubation period is 30 days. Young birds remain in the nest for about 13 weeks. Pet bird owners will be interested to know that there are a number of instances of Grey Parrots rearing young successfully in large cages indoors, and that many single females lay eggs.

Most people are familiar with Amazon parrots, the best-known being the Yellow-fronted and Blue-fronted, but few are aware that these birds are members of a large family. There are 26 species, only about eight of which are well-known in captivity. They have a wide distribution over Central and South America and the West

Indies. Some of those found only on small islands are, alas, in danger of extinction. That found on the island of Puerto Rico, for example, is probably the most critically endangered parrot in the world, next to the Kakapo from New Zealand, there being fewer than 30 individuals left.

Amazon parrots vary in size from about 27 to 45-cm. (10 to 15-in.). All those known to aviculturists are mainly green with contrasting colours on the head, primaries and tail. The Yellow-fronted, *Amazona ochrocephala ochrocephala*, for example, has yellow on the forehead and part of the crown and red on the shoulders and in the wings and tail.

Most Amazons will learn to repeat a few words, but only a few become really accomplished mimics. Yellow-fronted, Blue-fronted and Yellow-naped Amazons usually make the best talkers. Many Amazons learn to mimic the sounds they hear around them, human laughter being a favourite item in their repertoire. The favourite record of a pet Yellow-fronted in my possession is 'The Laughing Policeman' and she joins in at the right places.

Amazons are great fun to keep as pets if obtained when young. They usually become tame fairly quickly and like nothing better than to be carried around the house on their owner's shoulder. If allowed the freedom of the house, however, they are likely to get into all kinds of mischief and should only be let out under supervision.

There is a remarkable variation in character of Amazon parrots; some are completely trustworthy in temperament but most are liable to bite in moments of excitement. They are noisy, playful birds and should not be allowed to stay in a cage all day with nothing to amuse them. If a tame one is neglected it is liable to become noisy and spiteful. If the owner's circumstances change and he or she realises that the time is no longer available to devote to the bird, it is better to part with it to a sympathetic home before its temperament is completely spoiled.

However, it should also be pointed out that when male Amazons come into breeding condition, their character can change completely for a few weeks of the year, and they become treacherous, attacking even the most patient owner. For this reason, and because they are easier to handle, the smaller species such as the Orange-winged are particularly recommended as pets.

The Orange-winged, *A.amazonica,* is often confused with the Blue-fronted Amazon but it is much smaller, about 30-cm. (12-in.) and has a different arrangement of yellow and blue on the head. The markings in the tail and wings are orange, those of the Blue-front being red. The bill is horn-coloured.

The Blue-fronted Amazon, *A.aestiva,* is a bolder, more striking bird with black beak (and eyelashes). It measures about 36-cm. (14-in.).

A species which is an extremely popular pet in the U.S.A., where it is highly prized for its talking ability, but seldom available in Europe, is the Yellow-naped Amazon, *A.ochrocephala auropalliata.* This species is about the same size as the Blue-front and has a dark grey beak. There is a large patch of yellow on the nape, also on the crown in some birds. Its plumage otherwise resembles that of the Yellow-front.

A tame Amazon is one of the most delightful and amusing pets it is possible to own and, with luck and care, will give its owner many years of pleasure. Potentially, they are very long-lived and many have exceeded 50 years.

As aviary birds they have one fault which can prove embarrassing – their habit of screaming or shouting and chortling in the early morning and evening. Some birds are worse than others in this respect.

During recent years, Amazons have been bred with increasing regularity in captivity. Once again the main problem initially is in obtaining a true pair for, with a single exception, the plumage is alike in male and female.

Amazons lay two to four eggs, the larger species laying smaller clutches. Incubation is carried out by the female for 26 days and the young birds remain in the nest between eight and 10 weeks.

Rearing foods favoured by these birds include bread and milk and fresh vegetables, including corn-on-the-cob. As with African Greys, they will use a small barrel or a nest-box in which to breed. Large nest-boxes are unnecessary; Amazons in my possession measuring about 30-cm. (12-in.) in length, use boxes which are about 46-cm. (18-in.) high and 23-cm. (9-in.) square.

These birds and most large parrots delight in rain bathing, hanging from the roof of their aviary with wings outstretched to catch every drop of rain on their plumage. In this way they will keep in superb feather condition, unlike some caged parrots whose plumage looks dull and lifeless. It is extremely important to spray caged parrots at least two or three times weekly with warm water. In this way the natural gloss on their plumage will be retained. Alternatively, during warm weather, the cage can be placed outside during a shower of rain.

Parrots, especially cockatoos, give off a dust from their plumage which can aggravate such conditions in their owners as asthma. The dust is produced from a special type of feather known as powder-down which is found only in certain groups of birds. The barbs of such feathers continually disintegrate to produce a powder. This powder is used to clean the feathers and is responsible for the bloom on the plumage.

Exposure to water is absolutely essential to keep the plumage of birds from the humid tropics, such as macaws and amazons, in good condition. A fine spray of the kind used for house plants is therefore a useful item of equipment for the owner of a pet parrot.

A species which quite often used to be kept as a pet is the small Senegal Parrot, *Poicephalus senegalus.* This African species is relatively inexpensive, when available, but it is essential that a dark-eyed young bird is obtained if it is to be kept indoors. Imported adult birds are often extremely nervous and cannot be tamed.

The Senegal Parrot measures about 23-cm. (9-in.). It is mainly green, with the head grey and the abdomen orange or yellow. The beak is dark grey and the eye yellow. Plumage is alike in male and female. Young birds are much duller in colour.

Although small, this species often proves to be long-lived. There is a record of one pair which first nested in captivity when the male was known to be at least 40 years old and the female 25 years! This is another species which has successfully reared young indoors. Three or four eggs are laid and incubated by the female for 28 days.

In recent years the slightly smaller Meyer's Parrot from central and eastern Africa has been available almost as often as the Senegal (occasionally called 'African Green Parrot' or 'Green and Gold Parrot' by dealers) which is now imported less often than formerly.

Meyer's Parrot is mainly brown with the crown and shoulders yellow and the rump and underparts bluish-green. Its breeding habits and requirements are the same as the Senegal's. Neither

Bourkes Parakeet

Blue-winged Grass Parakeet

species needs a large aviary but both can prove fairly destructive for small birds.

A member of the same genus of unusual colour is Ruppell's Parrot, *P.ruppellii*, which is less often imported. It is mainly greyish-brown; the rump and upper tail coverts being tinged with blue in the male and bright blue in the female. The under wing coverts and thighs are yellow. Length is 23-cm. (9-in.).

About 28-cm. (11-in.) in length, of bolder build and very handsomely marked, is the Jardine's Parrot, *P. gulielmi*. It has a large strong beak and can prove rather destructive in an aviary. It is an attractive shade of dark green with most of the feathers of the upper parts edged with black. The forehead, bend of the wing and the thighs are marked with orange.

The aviculturist's inability to sex his birds correctly is often a major reason for breeding failure. There are no such problems with Eclectus Parrots. In the whole avian world there are very few species in which the male and female are so different in coloration; indeed for some years it was thought that they belonged to different species. What is more, these birds can be sexed from the time the feathers start to appear when they are four weeks old, so there is never any possibility of error.

Eclectus Parrots, *Eclectus roratus*, are found in New Guinea, Australia and Indonesia. The male is bright green and the female is mainly red. A true pair sitting together make an unforgettable sight. Not only are these birds beautifully coloured but they have a peculiar feather quality which is most attractive.

They are large, measuring in the region of 36-cm. (14-in.). Females are rather more stocky in build than males. The tail is of medium length and square.

Females vary in their coloration, according to their sub-species. The abdomen may be mauve or blue or entirely red; the wings are maroon and the head and breast are scarlet, also the under tail coverts. In some birds the under tail coverts, also the tip of the tail, is bright yellow. The beak is black.

In contrast, the male has the upper mandible orange, tipped with yellowish-white and the lower mandible black. His plumage is mainly green, with the sides red. The underside of the tail is black, narrowly tipped with yellow.

Young birds differ from adults only in their dark eyes and beak.

Eclectus are fascinating aviary birds, partly because once a compatible pair has been formed, they nest readily in captivity. The females are continuous breeders, that is, they have complete disregard for the seasons, and as soon as they have reared their young or discarded a clutch of eggs, they will lay again. I can stop my pair breeding only by removing the male for a while.

The major obstacle to be overcome is in finding a *compatible* pair. As in lovebirds and Ring-necked Parakeets, the female is dominant except during a brief period of courtship, and some males can never sufficiently overcome their fear of the dominant personality of the female. When a male and female are introduced, two feeding points in the aviary must be provided in case the female keeps the male away from the food. An attempt to do this may even by made by a long-established pair; if this happens, the female should be removed from the aviary for a while or the male may die through stress and starvation.

The clutch consists of two eggs which are incubated for 30 days by the female. Young birds emerge from the nest after about 12 weeks. Corn-on-the-cob is the main rearing food of my pair. They also take celery, peas, tomato, carrot, cheese and bread and milk. When the young are about three weeks old the adults start to eat seed, which is ignored until then.

Eclectus Parrots have a strange tendency to produce a preponderance of young of one sex. My own pair are a typical example: all the 10 young they have reared so far have been males.

Despite the fact that these birds do not start to breed until they are three or four years old, the wise aviculturist will obtain two young birds for breeding purposes because if they grow up together problems of incompatibility are less likely to arise. Aviary-bred birds are greatly to be preferred as newly imported birds can prove very difficult to establish.

Conure is the name given to certain parakeets from the neotropical countries. Most of those available will be imported birds as comparatively few are bred in captivity, some notable exceptions being the Nanday and the Sun Conures.

Conures are lively, inquisitive birds which make interesting aviary inhabitants and, if obtained when young, wonderful pets. Their major disadvantage is the voice, which is loud, harsh and penetrating. They need plenty of fruit in their diet, in addition to the usual seeds and greenfood.

One of the most beautiful species is the Sun Conure, *Aratinga solstitialis.* Until about 1971 it was extremely rare in aviculture but has since been established in captivity.

Words alone can give only a poor idea of its plumage which is fiery-orange on the head and underparts. The feathers of the mantle are yellow and orange and the upper wing coverts are green, tipped with yellow. The beak is black. This species measures about 30-cm. (12-in.), including the long tail. The plumage of immature birds is variable but usually has more green in the wings.

Sun Conures lay three or four eggs which are incubated by the female for 26 days. The young spend about eight weeks in the nest.

As in all conures, the plumage is alike in male and female. Regardless of sex, two birds will usually behave in an affectionate manner towards each other, spending most of the time close together and in mutual preening, thus conures are not easy birds to sex.

The Nanday Conure, *A.nenday,* has long been one of the most inexpensive and freely imported of the conures. It has a loud voice and thus is not everyone's favourite. It is immediately recognisable by its black head and red thighs; the rest of the plumage is green, dark above and paler below. It is about 33-cm. (13-in.) in length, including the long tail.

Nanday Conures nest very readily in captivity. Hand-reared youngsters make charming pets, being less noisy than wild caught birds and very affectionate.

The Golden-crowned Conure, *A.aurea,* has been bred in captivity on comparatively few occasions. It is most pleasingly marked, having the forehead and part of the crown orange, also the feathers surrounding the eye. The hind crown is blue, the rest of the upper parts being dark green; the underparts are yellowish-green. It measures about 25-cm. (10-in.). The black beak distinguishes it from the Petz's Conure, *A.canicularis,* which has the beak mainly horn-coloured and bare yellowish skin surrounding the eye. The latter is well-known as a pet bird in the U.S.A.

The Red-masked or Red-headed Conure, *A.erythrogenys,* is the most handsome of a group of conures which are predominantly green with red on the head. It has almost the entire head red, except the hind part of the cheeks, with scattered red feathers on the throat and bordering the head. The shoulders, edge of the wing, under wing coverts and thighs are also red. The beak is yellowish-white. Length is about 34-cm. (13-in.). Immature birds lack the red on the head when they are easily confused with other species. Obtained at this age, they make charming and intelligent pets.

The *Aratinga* conures form a large family; so do the *Pyrrhura* conures, some of which are extremely attractive aviary birds. Their voices are not quite as harsh and loud and they usually nest more readily and often prove prolific. It is not unusual for them to be double-brooded. Four to eight eggs are laid, according to the species, and incubated by the hen for 26 days. These birds invariably roost in their nest-boxes which must be left in position throughout the year. *Aratingas* vary in this respect; some use their boxes for roosting while others do not.

The most regularly imported of the *Pyrrhuras* is the Red-bellied Conure, *P. frontalis*. About 25-cm. (10-in.) long, it has a narrow reddish-brown band on the forehead and maroon on the abdomen and the underside of the long tail. Typically for this genus, the feathers of the sides of the neck and the upper breast contrast to the green body, being in this species yellowish edged with brown. The beak is black and there is a prominent area of white skin surrounding the eye. Immature birds resemble their parents but are slightly duller in colour.

Pyrrhuras are extremely inquisitive birds and excel in the art of finding their way out of the smallest hole. For this reason, their aviary must be carefully maintained to ensure that the wire or floor contains no holes.

The *Brotogeris* are small parakeets from South and Central America, which are mainly green with bright blue primaries and pointed tails. They have contrasting colours on the head or wings.

The best-known is the White-winged Parakeet, *B. versicolorus*. Young tame birds are often imported and would make charming pets if it were not for the harsh and persistent voice. The secondary coverts are yellow and when the wing is stretched or in flight it can be seen that some of the primaries and the primary coverts are also white. The bill is horn-coloured. This species measures about 22-cm. (9-in.). A sub-species known as the Canary-winged Parakeet, *B. v. chiriri*, is a prettier bird, being a purer shade of green and lacking the greyish tinge on the face.

The parakeets from New Zealand, often called Kakarikis, are as different as those from South America as can possibly be imagined. They are among the most active of all parrots and are therefore totally unsuited to life in a cage. Their long legs, ability to run up *and* down wire netting and their habit of scratching chicken-like in the ground distinguish them from all other parakeets.

Although they are extremely prolific breeders in captivity their life-span is seldom long. They have the ability to breed at an extremely early age and have been known to rear young when only five months old. However, it is advisable to wait until they are eight or nine months old before using them for breeding.

Kakarikis lay between five and nine eggs which are incubated by the female for 19 days. The chicks leave the nest when aged between six and seven weeks, by which time the female may already have laid the first egg of her next clutch. It is not unusual for a pair to rear a dozen young in one season, but they should be prevented from breeding during the winter as this could result in the female succumbing from egg-binding.

A fact which underlines the prolificacy of these birds is that in 1958 a census of Red-fronted Kakarikis in New Zealand aviaries gave the total as 103. Six years later there were over 2,500. The earlier low figure was due to the fact that it was not permissible to keep these birds in captivity until their declining numbers in the wild induced authorities to allow aviculturists to keep them.

The Red-fronted Kakariki, *Cyanoramphus novaezelandiae,* is mainly dark green with the forehead, crown and a small patch behind the eye crimson. A patch of this colour is found on each side of the rump. The flight feathers are dark blue and the beak is shiny bluish-grey. Length is about 28-cm. (11-in.). The eye is ruby red.

The Yellow-fronted New Zealand Parakeet or Kakariki, *C.auriceps,* is smaller, measuring about 23-cm. (9-in.). It is mainly green with the forehead red and the crown yellow. In both species the male is usually slightly larger and bolder in appearance with a larger head and beak.

Kakarikis require plenty of greenfood in their diet. In addition to the usual seeds, they also eat fruit and berries. When rearing young they should be offered bread and milk.

The Hanging Parrots, *Loriculus,* are a group of small birds from Asia and Indonesia. Their name is derived from their habit of sleeping hanging from the perch by the legs.

Their care in captivity is more like that accorded to a softbill than a parrot. Being inoffensive and not destructive to vegetation (except when nesting, when females cut leaves to carry into the nest), they are often kept in mixed collections of finches or other small birds. It is possible to keep them in a planted aviary and under these conditions they will often go to nest.

Losses with newly imported birds are high, thus it is worth paying more for established specimens. If caged during the acclimatisation period, the cage and perches will need to be cleaned very frequently because of their copious droppings and habit of flicking small pieces of fruit about. Layers of newspaper should be placed on the cage floor to absorb the liquid droppings. Bathing facilities or daily sprayings are essential if the birds' plumage is not to become sticky and soiled. Although beautiful and quiet, Hanging Parrots cannot be recommended as house pets, except for those who are prepared to spend some time cleaning up after them!

These small birds require a varied diet, the basis of which is fruit and nectar. Fruit such as apple and soft pear can be diced; grapes will also be relished and various soft fruits in season. Nectar, as previously described, should be offered, also sponge cake soaked in nectar. Some birds will eat small seeds such as canary seed and will enjoy spray millet.

Lack of breeding successes until fairly recent years was almost certainly due to an inadequate diet. Young are unlikely to be reared unless protein is available, either in the form of proprietary insectivorous mixtures, maggots (well cleaned), hard boiled egg, or eggfood manufactured for Canaries.

Hanging Parrots will nest in a small box or a log. The courtship behaviour of the male is interesting for the manner in which he feeds the female. Regurgitated food looks rather like bubble gum and is protruded from the beak for the female to suck up.

These birds lay three or four eggs which are incubated by the female for 20 days. Young remain in the nest for above five weeks.

The species most frequently imported is the Vernal Hanging Parrot, *L. vernalis*. It is mainly light green with the beak and the rump and tail coverts red and the throat blue. Length is about 13-cm. (5-in.). In some pairs it has been noted that the iris of the eye is white in the male and brown in the female.

Immature birds have the forehead and cheeks dull green, the

rump green and the bill pale orange. The eye is brown.

Appendix − Further Reading

In a book of this length it is not possible to cover in detail a group of birds whose requirements and characteristics are so varied. Suggestions for further reading are therefore given below:

Australian Parrakeets, Dr H.D. Groen − Groen, Holland
Encyclopedia of Cockatiels, George A. Smith − TFH Publications
Lories and Lorikeets, Rosemary Low − Paul Elek Ltd.
Lovebirds and the Related Parrots, George A. Smith − Paul Elek Ltd.
Parrots, Cockatoos and Macaws, E.J. Boosey − Barrie & Rockliffe (out of print, but worth making an effort to obtain)
Parrots of South America, Rosemary Low − John Gifford Ltd.

Index